gardening
with kids

Catherine Woram & Martyn Cox

gardening
with kids

photography by
Polly Wreford

RYLAND
PETERS
& SMALL

LONDON NEW YORK

Designer Iona Hoyle
Commissioning editor Annabel Morgan
Location researcher Emily Westlake
Production Paul Harding
Art director Leslie Harrington
Publishing director Alison Starling

First published in the United States in 2008
by Ryland Peters & Small
519 Broadway, 5th Floor
New York NY 10012
www.rylandpeters.com

10 9 8 7 6 5 4 3 2 1

ISBN: 978-1-84597-590-6

Library of Congress Cataloging-in-Publication Data

Woram, Catherine.
  Gardening with kids / Catherine Woram & Martyn
Cox ; photography by Polly Wreford.
      p. cm.
  Includes index.
  ISBN 978-1-84597-590-6
  1. Gardening--Juvenile literature. I. Cox, Martyn. II.
Title.
  SB457.W686 2008
  635--dc22
                                          2007042290

Printed in China.

contents

introduction	6
gardening with kids	8
growing	28
making	62
outdoor fun	114
suppliers	124
picture credits	126
index	127
acknowledgments	128

introduction

I've got my family to blame for my obsession with plants and gardens. As a toddler, I'd play with worms, make mud pies, or pluck rose petals from my mother's plants, mixing them with water to make my own perfume in old jelly jars. Later, I would learn about fruit and vegetables from my granddad, a fabulous gardener who would unearth potatoes before my eyes—as a child it was like seeing gold nuggets appearing from the earth! He gave me plump gooseberries and blackcurrants to eat, which made my eyes water, and let me pick peas straight from the plant. Even now, I can clearly remember the overpowering smell of the tomatoes that grew rampantly in his little greenhouse.

Enjoying being in the garden as a child, whether I was playing, picking vegetables, or growing plants in my own little patch of soil has stayed with me for life, and is a reason why I wanted to take up gardening for a living. Although few other kids will go on to become a professional, early exposure to gardening will sow the seed for a fascinating and rewarding hobby, and time spent outside is far healthier than sitting in front of the TV or computer screen.

Kids will love the many different projects in this book, which will expose them to lots of fabulous plants, from pretty flowers to curious insect eaters, and provide them with a gentle introduction to the technical skills needed to garden. The garden-related craft projects, meanwhile, will allow them to channel their creativity and keep them entertained on rainy days, when gardening is out of the question!

Both the growing and crafting projects are quick and easy, and fun to put together. Although some growing projects require a little patience (for plants or seeds to grow), most of the craft ones will yield instant results that kids will find encouraging. Here's to the next generation of green-thumbed gardeners!

Martyn Cox

gardening
with kids

gardening with kids

Before children arrive on the scene, we treat our gardens as adult-only spaces for outdoor entertaining and relaxing after a hard day at work. The minimalism of these gardens is unlikely to excite kids, but every garden, no matter how small, has the potential to be a fantastic playground.

Safety first

Although you may be lucky enough to have a garden that is already child-friendly, many gardens need a bit of a tweak, both in terms of safety and to make them more stimulating. If you have very young children, the most important thing is to make the garden a safe place. If you have ponds, fill them in until your kids are older. Alternatively, you could fence them off, or attach a decorative grille over the top.

Elsewhere, keep sheds or garages locked to prevent kids from gaining access to machinery, tools, or chemicals. For complete peace of mind, always be in the garden with them and keep a close eye on what they are doing.

Add some excitement

If you are planning a child-friendly garden or adapting your existing space, include plants that kids will find exhilarating. Large-leaved exotics, such as banana plants, make brilliant places to hide, while grasses and other tactile plants will become child magnets that just have to be touched and stroked whenever they head outdoors. Next on your list should be play equipment. A simple swing, sandbox, slide, or activity center will provide years of fun.

Give them their own patch

Find them a patch where they can grow their own vegetables, fruit, or flowers. Children like their independence and will get a thrill out of seeing their very own plants grow. To really give them ownership, help them to make a sign and paint their name on it, and let them manage the plot without your help or interference.

this page and opposite: getting green thumbs
If kids are exposed to the joys of gardening from a young age, they will soon become hooked. There are many elements of gardening that will appeal to kids—some will like watching seeds develop into a plant, while others will enjoy studying insects, and some children will just like getting their hands dirty!

Top tips on gardening with kids

- Give them a decent patch of soil where they can grow vegetables or flowers—not just the damp shady spot at the corner of the yard!

- Learn to relax, and let kids get mucky. It's fun!

- Teach them not to eat anything growing in the garden unless you are with them.

- For peace of mind with very young children, make sure there is no in-built danger, such as uncovered ponds or dangerous machinery left lying around. To prevent them from wandering off, make sure your gate is firmly shut and that there are no large gaps in the fence.

- Find space for play equipment and buy some outdoor games—these will provide hours of energetic fun.

- Turn your yard into an exciting jungle by adding some big, leafy exotics to your borders.

- Kids will want to spend all summer outdoors, so make sure they wear sun hats and reapply a high-factor sunscreen regularly. Bring them indoors when the sun is at its strongest—usually between 11 A.M. and 3 P.M.

- Kids love mini-beasts, so make wildlife habitats and encourage birds by putting out food.

- Try to keep an area of lawn. It's great for playing games, rolling around, or having picnics.

- Children are territorial, so give them their own set of garden tools to inspire them and get them started.

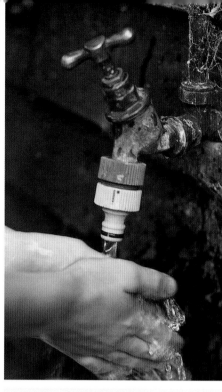

**this page and opposite above:
all kitted out**

Kids love being kitted out with pint-sized versions of the tools used by adults to maintain a garden. Look for scaled-down replicas that will fit snugly into a child's hand. Choose tools to suit the age of your children—plastic tools are perfect for toddlers, but older kids will prefer metal-bladed tools. When buying, check quality to make sure they will last.

getting started

Being given their first set of gardening equipment is a memorable experience for kids, and is the perfect way to encourage their interest in the garden. It can be great fun to go shopping together so they can help choose their own set of garden tools. The result will be tools they won't want to put down!

The starting point with any gardener, whatever their age, is to get equipped—you simply can't garden without the right tools. Fortunately, there are lots designed especially for kids and made from a variety of materials. Tough, round-edged miniature plastic tools are ideal for the very young, while longer-handled versions with stronger metal heads are perfect for older children. Most garden centers or hardware stores stock a good range, so it's not difficult to put together a kids' tool kit. Remember to keep it simple, as most gardening tasks can be carried out with a few tools (see box), and any special equipment can be bought as their interest develops.

Essential tool kit

Need to put a kids' gardening kit together? The important thing is to keep it simple, as most gardening can be carried out with a few key tools. Here are the essentials:

- hand trowel
- hand fork
- spade
- fork
- rake
- mini-wheelbarrow
- hoe
- garden scissors
- watering can
- broom

What to wear

Although kids can garden in old clothes, so it won't matter if they get dirty or damaged, it is still a good idea to provide them with some protective clothing. A pretty floral fabric or plastic gardening apron is perfect for girls, while boys (and some girls) may prefer an apron with a fun bug motif. A pair of brightly colored boots will keep their feet snug and dry, and kids should always wear a pair of gardening gloves whenever they handle soil or material like well-rotted compost. This will prevent them from picking up harmful bacteria, or diseases such toxoplasmosis, which is caused by decaying pet feces.

Storing equipment

As kids are quite territorial, give them somewhere they can store their tools. A brightly painted box in your shed or garage

this picture: giving it the boot!
A pair of boots is essential when kids are digging or splashing around in water. Children are attracted to boots in striking, primary colors or those with bold patterns printed on them—perfect for brightening up even the muddiest day.

would be ideal, especially if you (or they) paint their name onto it. Better still, give them complete ownership by finding space for a mini-shed or wooden playhouse in the yard, and allowing them to stash their garden equipment inside. You could even add plastic-coated hooks to the walls, so the tools can be neatly hung up after a session in the garden!

Preparing the soil

There is nothing more likely to deter a budding gardener than having their plants fail to grow. To make sure kids remain enthusiastic it is important to teach them how to prepare the soil properly, so seeds germinate and plants thrive.

Being given your own patch of soil is a rite of passage, and many adult gardeners started off with their own little patch, where they grew flowers or vegetables. Creating their own garden is tremendously empowering for kids, and, if given ownership of the plot, they will enjoy visiting it daily to carry out maintenance, such as watering or weeding, or to check on their plants.

If possible, give them a good piece of soil in a sunny spot, not a weedy patch in the shade where nothing will grow—the

idea is to encourage them, not disillusion them for life! Ideally, it should be within easy sight of the house, and not too large or they may struggle to care for it—a yard square would be the perfect size for beginners. Edge the area with pebbles, shells, bricks, or lengths of log, and mark their territory with a sign painted with their name.

Unless you've given them recently cultivated soil, it will need some work before planting in spring. Start by removing any weeds, then dig it over with a spade. Next, rake the soil to leave a fine finish and walk up and down on the soil with your heels to compact it. Then rake again, removing any large stones that have worked their way to the surface. Three weeks before planting or sowing seeds, improve the soil by spreading well-rotted farmyard manure

over the soil and work it into the surface with a fork (remember always to wear gloves when handling manure). The best time to prepare the soil is in the fall, but don't worry if you never got around to it— soil can still be prepared in spring.

Even if you only have a tiny yard or just a balcony, there's no need for your kids to be left out—the good news is that many compact varieties of fruit, vegetable, flowers, and herbs will thrive in containers filled with soil. See page 27 for a list of fun plants that can be grown in pots.

below and opposite: perfect preparations
If you are lucky enough to have a large yard, your children will take great pleasure in being given their own little patch. They will also enjoy the responsibility of thoroughly preparing the soil from scratch, which will enable them to successfully grow a selection of their favorite fruit, vegetables, and flowering plants.

this page and opposite: taking care of your soil

Many adults don't bother looking after their garden soil, considering it to be a bit of a chore, but kids will benefit from the exercise and revel in nurturing their patch of ground. If they are taught that improving the soil means their plants will grow better, they will happily spend time preparing the soil. Teach your kids to dig over the ground, to boost the soil by adding well-rotted manure, to weed, and to water, or to make their own compost by collecting kitchen waste and prunings. All of this work will pay handsome dividends when it comes to harvesting or flowering time, and they will want to do it all over again the following year.

Maintaining the garden

With a little bit of tender loving care, a garden will flourish, providing positive results that will fill kids with enthusiasm. From learning how to water properly to making a compost pile, kids will enjoy picking up the simple techniques needed to maintain their space.

Watering

Every plant needs water to keep it in good shape, but there is no simple "one size fits all" rule, since every plant and garden situation is different. Generally, make sure that plants do not dry out, especially seedlings or plants in pots, which will soon wilt when their roots have drawn every last drop from the soil. While plants are actively growing or bearing flowers or fruit, you may need to water daily, or even twice a day for some thirsty containers, such as hanging baskets. Let kids water their plants with a watering can with a fine rose attachment—this gives a soft trickle, rather than an earth-boring torrent of water.

Feeding

Garden centers are full of dozens of different fertilizers, but the best thing to do in a kid's garden is keep the feeding regime very simple and easy to follow. All they really need is a liquid feed that's high in potassium, such as tomato fertilizer. This can then be added to water and poured onto plants to boost flower, fruit, or vegetable production.

Mulching

A great trick to reduce the need for watering on permanent plantings of shrubs, perennials, and trees (but not around seedlings or vegetables) is to spread a thick carpet of bark chips or other organic material across the surface of the soil. Called a mulch, this thick layer prevents moisture from escaping from the soil, as well as looking good and preventing weeds from growing. You can use a similar technique with pots, covering the surface of the soil with shells, pine cones, pebbles, or smooth tumbled pieces of colored glass.

Composting

You end up with a lot of waste in the garden, so show your kids how grass cuttings, prunings, and dead flower heads can be turned into compost. Add organic material in layers to the bin of your choice, and within months the spent material will have magically turned into compost. In a small yard, try a worm bin—these can be bought as kits and are ideal for most garden waste and vegetable peelings from the kitchen.

Pest control

To us they are annoying pests, but many very young kids think of slugs, snails, and other leaf-munching beasties as cute garden pets—some even give them names and keep them in small boxes. Obviously, you do not want all of their hard work to go to waste, so a degree of control (ideally when they are not looking!) is necessary. In the long run, it's probably best to take a tip from organic gardeners and learn to live with a few pests.

growing and planting

Many adults have started a lifelong fascination with gardening when young, raising beansprouts on blotting paper or by sowing the seeds from an apple core in the soil. Growing from seed is a magical experience for children, especially if you use fast-growing seeds that pop up in just a few days.

Sprouting seeds

Cast your mind back to your school days, and you may recall a basic lesson in botany when a teacher showed the class how seeds germinate. He or she would moisten a bean seed and drop it into a glass jar, while you would check it daily to see whether it had produced any roots or shoots.

Watching seeds germinate fascinates children, largely because it demystifies a process that usually takes place underground, letting them see how plants grow. It is incredibly easy to try this at home. Simply roll up a piece of paper towel into a cylinder and put it inside an old glass jar. Moisten a bean seed (perfect, because they are fast-growing) and place halfway down the side of the jar, sandwiched between the paper and the glass. Pour some water into the jar and the paper towel will soak it up to hold the bean in place. Within a few days, you will notice the beans swell. This will lead to the seed coat's cracking and the roots appearing, later followed by the slowly unfurling shoot that carries the leaves.

Even more fun are edible sprouting seeds, which can be grown in a jar or a special sprouting device. Alfalfa, beet, chickpeas, lentils, mung beans, and fenugreek are ideal, will appear in a day or so, and are perfect for adding a crunch to salads or sandwiches.

Planting from seed

Seeds are simple to grow, whether you decide to buy seed packs from a garden center or collect your own from seed heads in the garden (check that the plants aren't poisonous before letting children gather them). All you need to do is fill a pot with potting mix, firm it down gently to leave a level surface, and then scatter the seeds on top. Cover with soil (how much depends on the size of the seeds, so check the back of the seed pack for information), water, and put them in a light place to germinate. Many seeds will

this picture, left and far left: sprouting beans
Moistened beans will germinate quickly and form a large, spreading root that will anchor the seed to the ground and absorb moisture from the paper towel, allowing the seed to put its energy into producing a slender shoot bearing leaves.

above and right: sowing seeds
Children love to choose seeds from the massive selection in garden centers. It's also fun to save your own seeds. Show kids how to collect them from drying flower heads and store them in envelopes for sowing next year.

above and opposite: simple cuttings

Propagating succulent plants is fun and foolproof. Cut off a length of stem and put in a pot filled with gritty potting mix—it should root within weeks. Kids will enjoy making paper pots for cuttings with a pot-maker device.

left: repotting seedlings

It's easy to germinate seeds in the same pot, but as they grow into seedlings, they will need a pot of their own so they don't have to compete for nutrients and water. Remove the seedlings carefully, handling the roots gently, and replant them at the same depth as before.

germinate more quickly if they are popped into a windowsill propagator, but don't worry if you haven't got one—a clear plastic freezer bag placed over the pot and secured with a rubber band will work just as well, and can be removed after the seeds have germinated. When the seedlings are large enough (several weeks later), they can be allowed to develop fully by giving them a pot of their own.

Buying plants

Raising plants from seed is great when you have fast-growing flowers or vegetables, or have patient kids who don't mind waiting several months for plodding plants to reach their peak. However, if you want to cheat or are itching to grow a plant that you can't raise from seed, buy them from a nursery, garden center, or online specialist.

Go for plants that are vigorous, healthy, and have no visible signs of pests and diseases. It also pays to be sneaky and lift the plant out of the pot to check its roots—if the rootball is a mass of congested roots that are spiraling round and round, put it back—pot-bound plants will have been in the container for a very long time, and the roots may fail to anchor the plant securely when planted. The perfect plant will fill the pot, but the roots won't be circling.

Planting

Although some plants are fussy, when it comes to planting you generally need to prepare a roundish hole that is slightly deeper and wider than the rootball. The surface of the rootball should sit at the same level as the surface of the soil. Remove the plant from its pot, put it in the hole, and add or remove soil as necessary. Firm the soil, and water well after planting.

Taking easy cuttings

An alternative to buying plants is to let kids grow plants themselves by taking simple cuttings. Perhaps the most foolproof plants to try this out on are indoor succulents. All you need to do is snap a healthy leaf from a plant, and rest on the edge of a small pot filled with gritty potting mix. The cut end will soon form roots in the soil, followed by a new plant.

choosing plants

To nurture a child's interest in gardening, it's essential to let them get involved in picking plants for the garden. Growing varieties they have selected—with your help, to make sure they'll suit your garden—will help to give them a sense of ownership, and they'll love caring for them.

Visiting the garden center is a great adventure for kids, but for adults the endless benches crammed with so many plants can cause a serious amount of head-scratching. The tempting selection on offer will often result in random impulse buys, and it's only when we get home that we realise our garden can't provide the conditions the new plant requires.

Plants to suit your garden

There's nothing more disheartening than buying a new plant only for it to turn up its toes after being planted. To make sure plants thrive, choose ones that are suited to the conditions in your garden, whether it's in full sun or plunged in shade for much of the day. Equally important is to choose plants that will grow in your soil, whether it's clay or sandy, acidic or limey. Of course, there are ways of cheating—if you want to grow a plant that you know won't like your soil, you could always grow it in a container.

What to buy

There's little point filling the garden with delicate varieties that are easily damaged by inquisitive fingers or an errant football. Go for tough plants, so that children can touch, stroke, or even scrunch up the leaves with their hands. Bananas, leathery elephant's-ears, or soft, downy lamb's ears are all ideal and are able to cope with this kind of attention. Very young children will love to grow flowers in bright, primary colors, while slightly older kids will enjoy choosing and growing edible plants, which, apart from tasting great, will also help them understand about the origin of food.

What not to grow

There are loads of plants that kids can be encouraged to grow, but there are also several that are best avoided (see box opposite). Many well-known garden plants are poisonous, have vicious spikes, or are covered in tiny hairs that cause irritation to the skin when touched. Teach children what they can or can't touch and, as a general rule of thumb, don't let them eat anything without asking permission first.

this page and opposite: decisions, decisions Head to your nearest garden center, nursery, or hardware store and you will find shelves packed with fabulous plants. To nurture children's interest in gardening, get them involved in choosing plants. Growing varieties they have helped select (with help, to make sure they'll suit your garden) will give them a sense of ownership, and they'll love to care for them.

What not to grow

These plants should be avoided when gardening with kids.

- *Aconitum* (monkshood)
- *Alstroemeria*
- *Brugmansia* (angel's trumpet)
- Castor-oil plant
- *Delphinium*
- *Echium* (viper's bugloss)
- *Euphorbia*
- Foxglove
- Giant hogweed
- *Laburnum*
- Lupine
- *Nerium oleander* (oleander)
- Rue
- *Solanum*
- *Zantedeschia* (calla lily)

above left and right, and left: beautiful but deadly
They are beautiful to look at, but lupine, foxglove, money plant, and many other plants have poisonous seeds, berries, flowers, or leaves, and are best not grown in a child-friendly garden.

plant lists

With thousands of plants available, it can be difficult to decide what to grow. To make life easier, here are lists of plants that are child-friendly and will appeal to kids of all ages. Whether you've got a large garden or just a windowbox, there are some great plants to try. Check for your zone when you shop.

Salad-bowl garden
- Lettuce 'Lollo Rosso'
- Spinach 'Bordeaux' (red stem, baby leaf)
- Lettuce 'Mizuna'
- Scallion
- Cherry tomato 'Tumbler'
- Corn salad 'Pepite'
- Cucumber
- Lettuce 'Little Gem'
- Mache
- Edible carrot leaf (grown for leaves, not roots)
- Mustard
- Radish
- Beet 'Bulls Blood' (grown for its leaves)
- Tatsoi

left: funny face
Kids will love to make a funny face or pretty pattern out of the salad-bowl plants, fruit, berries, and vegetables that they have grown in the garden. An old wooden seed tray, first lined with plastic and then filled with sand, will make a perfect frame for their home-grown edible designs.

Crazy fruit and vegetables
- Brussels sprouts 'Red Delicious' (purple sprouts)
- Chard 'Bright Lights' (mix of white, red, pink, gold and orange stems)
- Strawberry 'Maxim' (fruit as big as a small hand)
- Tomato 'Tigerella' (stripy fruit)
- Squash 'Turks Turban'
- Borlotti bean 'Lamon' (pink and white blotched pods and mottled beans)
- French bean 'Purple King' (dwarf purple beans)
- Cucumber 'Crystal Lemon' (round, yellow fruit)
- Eggplant 'Mohican' (white fruit)
- Carrot 'Purple Haze' (purple carrots)
- Sweetcorn 'Indian Summer' (white, red, purple, and yellow kernels on the same cob)
- Sweetcorn 'Red Strawberry' (for popcorn)
- Raspberry 'Allgold' (golden raspberries)
- Beet 'Chioggia' (cut it open to reveal white and red concentric rings)
- Zucchini 'One Ball' (round, orange fruit)

above: scaring the birds

After growing lots of delicious edible plants, the last thing you want is for greedy birds to take a share of your children's yummy crops! Try making a fun scarecrow, or suspend a string of CDs above the plants—you can use the free ones that are often given away with newspapers and magazines.

Fast-growing seeds

- Radish
- Carrot Parmex
- Arugula
- Cress
- Spinach
- Turnip Arcoat
- Beet Pronto
- *Nigella* 'Miss Jekyll' (love-in-a-mist)
- *Limnanthes* (fried-egg plant)
- Nasturtium
- *Eschscholzia* (California poppy)
- *Cerinthe major* (honeywort)
- *Cosmidium*
- Sunflowers
- Annual poppies (not opium poppy)

Scratch and sniff

- *Stachys byzantina* (lamb's ears)
- *Salvia officinalis* 'Icterina' (variegated sage)
- *Salvia argentea* (wooly leaves)
- *Bergenia* (elephant ears)
- *Stipa tenuissima* (feather grass)
- *Melianthus major* (blue leaves that smell of peanut butter)
- *Briza maxima* (quaking grass)
- Thyme
- Basil
- *Antennaria* (cat's-ear)
- *Helichrysum italicum* subsp. *serotinum* (curry plant)
- *Bellis perennis* cultivars (daisy)
- *Callistemon* (bottlebrush)
- *Convolvulus cneorum* (soft, silver leaves)
- *Coprosma* (shiny, glossy leaves)
- Bronze fennel (feathery foliage)

Giant's garden

- *Musa basjoo* (hardy banana)
- *Hosta* 'Big Daddy'
- Bamboo
- Tree fern
- *Fatsia japonica*
- Cardoon
- *Melianthus major* (honey bush)
- *Tetrapanax papyriferum* (rice paper plant)
- Pole beans (on wigwams)
- *Macleaya cordata* (plume poppy)
- *Verbena bonariensis*
- *Helianthus* 'Lemon Queen'
- *Dahlia imperialis* (tree dahlia)
- x *Fatshedera lizei*

above: water works
Children will be encouraged if the plants they grow thrive and flourish, rather than just limp along before turning brown and dying. Water is essential for a lush, verdant garden. To keep everything they grow in good health, encourage your kids to water plants plentifully after planting, and let them check whether plants need watering on a daily basis.

Nature's garden

- *Buddleia* (butterfly bush)
- *Hebe*
- *Veronica*
- *Leucanthemum vulgare* (ox-eye daisy)
- Pole beans
- *Dipsacus fullonum* (teasel)
- Forget-me-not
- *Stipa tenuissima* (feather grass)
- Sunflower
- Lavender
- Marigold
- *Nepeta* (catnip)
- Fennel
- *Sedum spectabile*
- Marjoram
- Rosemary
- Thyme
- Chives

Plants for pots

- Pansies and violets
- *Petunia*
- *Begonia*
- Nasturtium
- *Sempervivum* (houseleeks)
- Marigold
- *Pelargonium*
- *Cosmos atrosanguineus* (chocolate cosmos)
- *Fuchsia*
- *Brassica oleracea* (ornamental cabbage)
- *Lagurus ovatus* (hare's tail grass)
- *Solenostemon* (coleus)
- *Pennisetum* 'Purple Majesty'
- Heathers
- Box topiary shapes

this page: insect appeal
It's a great idea to turn your garden into a nature reserve by encouraging beneficial mini-beasts. Many plants (such as those listed on the "Nature's garden" plant list above), garden features, or feeding stations will act like magnets for ladybugs, butterflies, bees, birds, and even small mammals, such as chipmunks, and will allow your children to observe all these little creatures at close range.

growing

herb planter

Growing herbs is a great way to learn about edible plants, and they're a breeze to grow in a window box on a sunny window ledge or patio. For a never-ending supply of tasty leaves, all you need to do is to keep picking them!

WHAT YOU WILL NEED
- large terracotta window box
- stones or large pieces of broken terracotta
- potting mix
- small trowel
- selection of herbs to fill your trough (we used chives, rosemary, mint, oregano, and thyme)
- watering can

1. Cover holes

Before filling your window box with soil, cover the drainage holes in the base. Use large stones or pieces of broken terracotta pot. This will allow water to drain away but prevent the holes from getting clogged up with soil. It will also stop soil from spilling out through the holes and onto surfaces.

2. Add potting mix

Cover the base of your container with ½ inch (1 cm) of potting mix, breaking up any clods with your hands. Roughly level with your fingers to leave a smooth finish.

3. Arrange plants

Take your plants out of their containers and arrange them in the window box. Upright plants will look better in the center of the container, while creeping plants are best tumbling over the ends. Once you are happy with your display, fill the gaps around the plants with soil, leaving a level surface about an inch below the top of the trough. Firm around the plants with your fingertips and water them well.

HINTS AND TIPS

- Harvest your herbs regularly to keep the plants productive.
- Always keep the container well watered—don't let it dry out.
- Chives, tarragon, parsley, rosemary, mint, sage, and thyme are all perfect for growing in window boxes or troughs.

harvesting herbs

During late spring and summer, herbs make lots of fresh new growth, which is perfect for harvesting and drying. Store dried herbs in cellophane bags, and keep them handy in the kitchen. They also make great presents to give to friends.

1. Cut herbs

Select a handful of fresh, healthy new shoots and snip them off with a pair of scissors. To make sure the parent plant is left in good shape, cut just above a pair of leaves. Fill a bowl with cold water and quickly dip the shoots to remove any dirt, then gently dry them on a paper towel.

2. Prepare to dry

Cover a tray with a sheet of waxed paper and lay the shoots on top to dry. If you are drying different herbs, make sure they are not touching. Now put the tray in a warm, dark cupboard until the herbs have dried completely.

3. Finishing

Carefully remove the individual leaves and put them into small cellophane bags. Fold over and secure the top of the bag to keep the contents fresh. Add a label, then store the herbs in a kitchen cupboard.

HINTS AND TIPS
- Herbs take several weeks to dry. You will know they are ready when they snap easily, which means there is no moisture left in the leaves.
- Rosemary, bay, thyme, sage, marjoram, tarragon, basil, and parsley are all ideal for drying.
- You can also finely chop herbs and freeze them in an ice-cube tray. Top them up with water and put the tray in the freezer.

crazy eggheads

Creating these cute eggheads is really easy and fun. Fill them with fast-growing seed, then give the "hair" a trim in a few days' time. You can add the yummy sprouts to salads and sandwiches!

WHAT YOU WILL NEED
- hard-boiled eggs
- knife
- pencil
- absorbent cotton
- water
- quick-growing seeds
- teaspoon

optional:
- egg carton • popsicle sticks • paint and paintbrush • glue

1. Prepare eggs
Remove the top from a hard-boiled egg by gently tapping around the outside of the shell with a knife (make a hole that is large enough for you to extract the egg). Scoop out the egg with a teaspoon.

2. Draw on face
Hold the shell gently, and draw a face on the outside with a pencil. Don't press too hard, or you might break the shell.

3. Add cotton
Gently push a handful of absorbent cotton into the eggshell. Pour in a little water and let the cotton soak it up.

4. Sow seed

Sow a generous teaspoonful of seed over the surface of the damp cotton (we used cress and purple radish seeds). If you want, finish the eggheads by using colorful paints to define the face you drew earlier. Now you can sit back and watch the crazy "hair" grow, but remember to water the seeds every day so they don't dry out.

HINTS AND TIPS

• Make a body and feet for your egghead by cutting out a cup from a cardboard egg carton and using strong glue to attach short lengths of popsicle stick underneath. Paint them in jolly colors.

• Cut the "hair" with scissors when it's about 2 inches (5 cm) long.

• You can also try growing super-fast red radish, mustard, garlic chives, and alfalfa sprouts. Mmm!

potato planter

Whether you like them mashed, roasted, or baked, potatoes are an easy vegetable to grow in a large container. Plant seed potatoes in spring, and you'll soon be unearthing masses of tasty tubers.

WHAT YOU WILL NEED
- large planter, at least 12 inches wide and deep (we used a metal wastebasket)
- multi-purpose potting soil
- 3 x potato tubers per pot

2. Sprout potatoes

When you buy your seed potatoes in late winter, you need to sprout them before planting. Place a single potato into the hollow of a cardboard egg carton, making sure that the end with the most eyes (little indents where buds will grow) faces upward. Put in a light, cool place until the sprouts are about an inch (2.5 cm) high. This stage may take up to six weeks.

1. Prepare pot

Most pots have holes in their base to allow excess water to drain away, preventing the growing potatoes from rotting. If yours doesn't, ask an adult to drill some in the base.

3. Plant sprouted potatoes

Add a 4-inch (10-cm) layer of soil to your planter, stand a sprouted tuber on top with the sprouts pointing up, and cover it with another 4-inch (10-cm) layer of soil. Water well. When the potato shoots are about 6 inches (15 cm) tall (which will take several weeks), cover the stems with soil, allowing the tips to just poke above the surface. As the stems grow, add more soil until you are left with a 4-inch (10-cm) gap between the surface of the soil and top of the pot.

4. Harvest potatoes

Your potatoes will be ready for picking in midsummer, after the plants have flowered. Loosen the soil with your hands and pull the plants up. There should be plenty of potatoes attached to the roots and more hidden in the soil.

HINTS AND TIPS

• Potatoes will thrive in a warm and sunny spot.

• Keep plants well watered—never let the soil dry out.

• It's essential to keep on adding soil to cover the growing shoots, or your potatoes will be green and inedible.

• There are lots of potato varieties available, some of which produce larger tubers that need to stay in the soil until late summer.

butterfly basket

Bees and butterflies are good for the garden, and it's easy to attract them by planting a hanging basket full of their favorite flowers. Choose a sunny spot and hang from the branch of a tree or a bracket attached to the wall of your house.

WHAT YOU WILL NEED
- hanging basket (with a liner and a chain for hanging)
- multi-purpose soil
- watering can

plants:
- 1 x French lavender
- 3 x fuchsia
- 3 x convolvulus
- 3 x marigold
- 3 x alyssum

1. Add soil
Make sure the basket liner has holes in the bottom for drainage—make some, if necessary. Put a layer of soil in the bottom of the basket, breaking up any clods with your hands.

2. Start planting
Put the large lavender plant in the center of the basket. Add or remove soil as needed, so there is a gap of about an inch (2.5 cm) between the surface of the rootball and the lip of the basket.

3. Pot-bound plants
Plants with a mass of congested roots will not be able to anchor themselves in the soil and will grow poorly. Tease the roots of pot-bound plants apart gently before planting them.

4. Finish planting

Plant your first fuchsia at the edge of the basket. Repeat with the two remaining fuchsias, spacing them evenly around the edge. Finish by planting one convolvulus, marigold, and alyssum in each of the three remaining spaces. Firm the plants down well and plug any gaps with soil.

5. Water plants

To give your butterfly basket a flying start, water it well using a watering can with a rose. This will spread water evenly across the container without eroding a hole in the soil.

HINTS AND TIPS

• Why not try some different plants in your basket? Bees and butterflies will also flock to veronica, hebe, bugle, cornflower, thrift, ageratum, heather, and thyme.

• Make sure to water the basket regularly to prevent the soil from drying out—up to twice a day during hot weather.

• You can keep the display going for longer by pinching off any fading flowers with your fingers.

butterfly basket   39

strawberry planter

Picking plump and juicy strawberries is a summer treat, and it's easy to grow your own in a special strawberry planter. For lots of berries, put the planter in a sunny spot and keep it well watered.

1. Add soil
Cover the drainage hole at the bottom of the pot with a stone to stop it from clogging. Add soil to just below the level of the first pocket and pat down with your fingers.

2. Plant strawberries
Remove a plant from its pot and put it into a pocket. Push soil around the roots, but don't cover the crown of the plant (where the shoots come from the soil).

3. Finish planting
Add more soil and plant the other pockets. Finish off by putting a strawberry plant in the top and fill the gaps around it with soil. Leave a 1-inch (2.5-cm) gap between the top of the soil and the lip of the pot.

4. Water plants
Water well, so the roots are soaked. Water the top of the planter, not each pocket, as you could wash the soil out and expose the roots.

colorful annuals

Annuals will fill your garden with cheerful color. Buy them as plants in early summer and they will flower non-stop until the fall. For a really fun, jazzy display, use your imagination and plant them in the most unusual containers you can find.

1. Add soil
Put a generous handful of soil in the bottom of a container. Don't worry about drainage holes, as annual plants only last for a short time.

2. Plant up
Sit a plant on top of the soil. The surface of the rootball needs to be just beneath the lip of the pot, so add or remove soil as necessary.

HINTS AND TIPS
• Before buying plants, make sure they'll fit your containers.
• Make plants flower longer by pinching off blooms as they fade.
• Plants in small pots will need water more often than those in larger containers. During hot, dry weather, you may need to give plants a drink twice a day.
• Use pebbles or shells to dress the surface of containers. This helps the soil retain water.

3. Finishing
Use more soil to fill any gaps around the edges of the rootball and firm down with your fingertips. Water plants, but don't overdo it, as the beaker doesn't have drainage holes. Add some water, let it soak in, then test by pushing your finger into the soil. If it's thoroughly wet, you don't need to add any more.

1. Buy plants

You can find lots of jazzy annuals in the garden center, including sunflowers, petunias, impatiens, pansies, violas, dahlias, and marigolds. Buy a selection of the most striking flowers you can find to make a colorful splash in the garden.

2. Choose containers

Use your imagination and plant up lots of different types of container. Old teapots, jugs, saucepans, and many other items found in the kitchen or around the house are ideal, and they can be arranged together to create an eye-catching display.

crystallized pansies

Real flowers make the prettiest of decorations for cupcakes, and they taste good, too. Egg white and superfine sugar is all that is needed to create these pretty crystallized flowers.

WHAT YOU WILL NEED

- fresh pansies
- plate
- paintbrush
- whites of two eggs
- superfine sugar
- cupcakes
- cake plate or cakestand

1. Paint on egg white

Using a fine paintbrush, carefully paint each flower with egg white. Paint no more than seven or eight flowers at a time, as the egg white dries quickly.

2. Sprinkle on sugar

Use a spoon to sprinkle superfine sugar over the flowers, making sure not to add too much sugar. Leave to dry. The flowers will become hard and brittle.

HINTS AND TIPS

- There are many edible flowers, including roses and nasturtiums.
- Pick the flowers on a dry day—if they are damp, they will get mushy
- Pregnant women, elderly people, and young children should avoid raw egg whites.

3. Finishing

Use two or three of the flowers to decorate each cupcake. Serve on a pretty cake plate or glass cake stand.

cacti planter

Cacti are bizarre-looking plants that are covered in spines that help protect them from predators in their native environment. Many come from desert regions of the world, and it's great fun making your own miniature desert landscape by growing several plants together. Cacti are virtually indestructible, as long as they are given a light spot indoors and an occasional watering.

1. Apply undercoat
Apply a coat of white undercoat to the bowl, making sure that all the terracotta is evenly covered. It's easiest to paint the inside first. Then, when it's dry, turn the bowl over to paint the sides and base.

2. Paint overcoat
When the undercoat is completely dry, paint the bowl your chosen color. Start with the inside, let it dry completely, then turn it over and paint the sides and base. For the best results, apply a second coat after the first is dry.

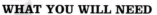

WHAT YOU WILL NEED

- large terracotta pot or bowl with a drainage hole in the base
- undercoat
- paint in your chosen color
- three additional paint colors for decorative stripes
- paintbrushes
- stones or pieces of broken terracotta pot
- special cacti potting mix
- small trowel
- cacti (enough to fill your container)
- gloves
- strip of cardboard
- white gravel
- watering can

3. Add stripes

Jazz up your bowl by adding some stripes. We painted three concentric bands against the yellow background, using the ridges molded into the bowl as a guide. Let it dry completely.

4. Fill with potting mix

Cover the hole in the base of the bowl with a piece of broken pot or stone to prevent it becoming blocked. Start to fill with the special potting mix. Leave an inch (2.5 cm) between the surface of the soil and the lip of the pot and firm with your fingertips.

cacti planter 47

5. Lifting cacti

Cacti are covered in tiny spines, so you need to pick up the plants carefully. When you are handling them, wear tough gloves and remove the plants from their pots by bending a strip of cardboard and clamping it around them. This way, you can pick up the cacti safely without getting spiked!

6. Plant cacti

Using a trowel, make planting holes in the soil. The plant's rootball needs to sit at the same level as the surface of the soil. Lower each cactus into its hole and fill any gaps with soil. Gently press down the soil with your fingertips.

7. Add gravel

Water the plants, then cover the entire surface with decorative gravel. We used white chips, but you could use polished pebbles, sand, or crushed shells. Spread a thick layer, which sits just beneath the rim of the pot.

HINTS AND TIPS

• From the middle of fall to the end of winter, water the cacti every three weeks, while from late spring to the end of summer, water when the soil starts to dry out.

• Many cacti enjoy bright sunshine, so put your cacti planter in the brightest spot possible, especially in winter, when light levels dip.

alpine garden

Tiny alpine plants originate from mountainous parts of the world, where they thrive in well-drained soil among the rocks. It's easy to create your own miniature landscape by planting a selection of these mini-marvels in an old ceramic sink or a plastic trough.

1. Choose plants
Garden centers stock a large range of diminutive alpine plants. Choose a selection of flowering and foliage plants, and buy enough to spread across your sink. Don't buy too many, as you want to leave gaps between plants. We used ten plants, but you may need more or less depending on the size of your sink.

2. Add soil
Cover the drainage hole with a piece of broken terracotta pot or a stone, to allow drainage but prevent the hole from becoming blocked. Next, spread a layer of soil over the bottom of the sink.

3. Arrange plants
Arrange your plants, still in their pots, in the sink. If your container is to go against a wall, put big plants at the back and creeping varieties at the front to cascade down the sides. Small groups of plants often look best grouped together, such as the yellow saxifrages here.

4. Planting

Place the pieces of tufa in the sink. They look best partially buried in the soil. Start planting in one corner, working your way across. Dig planting holes, insert the plants, then fill the space around each plant with soil. Leave a 1-inch (2.5-cm) gap between the surface of the soil and the top of the sink.

HINTS AND TIPS

- Old sinks are very heavy, so plant yours in its final position—plants will do best in full sun or partial shade.
- As flowers begin to fade, pinch them off between your fingers.
- Alpine gardens look great when the plants merge, but you may need to thin out vigorous plants to prevent them from taking over.

5. Cover surface

After planting, add a blanket of horticultural grit to the surface. Not only does this look good, but it also prevents weeds from growing and helps the soil retain moisture. If you spill grit onto the plants, you can remove it with a soft paintbrush. Now give each plant a good, long drink of water.

succulent tower

Houseleeks are the ultimate low-maintenance plant, as they don't need watering, pruning, or any special care at all. They make a great feature for a patio when grown in a tower of different-sized terracotta pots—try painting your pots first with exterior paint in your favorite color.

WHAT YOU WILL NEED
- large, medium, and small terracotta pots (we used 16-inch (40-cm), 10-inch (25-cm), and 6-inch (13-cm) pots
- house brick
- stones or pieces of broken pot
- gritty potting mix (a mix of 50 percent potting mix and 50 percent horticultural grit)
- houseleeks (two different colors and a large-leafed variety for the top of the tower)
- horticultural grit

1. Make base pot stable
Put a brick in the bottom of the largest pot to prevent the hole in the base of the pot from clogging up and to give the tower extra stability. Fill the gap around the brick with soil and pack it down.

2. Stack second pot
Place the second pot on top of the first and put a stone or piece of broken pot over the drainage hole. About a quarter of the pot should sit below the lip of the first. Fill the top of the base pot with soil up to about an inch below the lip of the pot.

3. Add top pot
Add the last pot so a quarter of it will be buried when soil is added. Cover the drainage hole with a piece of pot, then fill in the gap with soil and pack it down. Now fill a third of the top pot with soil.

4. Add plants
Plant the first level with one type of houseleek. Make a hole with your finger and push the roots in. Plant the next layer, and finish with the largest plant at the top.

HINTS AND TIPS

• Large, well-grown houseleeks can be split apart into individual rosettes for planting—one plant may be enough for a layer of your tower. Simply tease the rosette away from the main plant, making sure there's a piece of stem and roots attached.

• Houseleeks spread by forming new rosettes—over time, they will cascade over the sides of the pot.

5. Spread grit

Spread grit around each plant so the soil is covered. This prevents weeds from growing and keeps the bottom leaves of the plant dry so they don't rot.

terrarium

You don't need a garden to grow lots of plants. Small houseplants can be planted together in large glass jars to make an eye-catching display that needs very little watering or care. These gardens in a bottle look great on a windowsill or shelf.

WHAT YOU WILL NEED
- glass container (we used a Mason jar)
- clay pellets
- horticultural charcoal
- multi-purpose potting mix
- long-handled spoon
- a selection of plants (enough for your container)
- watering can

1. Add clay pellets
Make sure the inside of the glass is clean (so you can see the plants!) and then slowly pour in your expanded clay pellets to make a 2-inch (5-cm) drainage layer covering the base of the jar.

2. Pour in charcoal
Permanently damp soil can become smelly, so add a thin layer of horticultural charcoal over the clay pellets, which will keep it fresh.

3. Fill with soil
Fill a quarter of the container with soil and firmly press it down with your fingers (if your wrist can't fit through the neck of the bottle, use the back of a long-handled spoon to press the soil down).

5. Water plants

Pour water gently into the jar until the soil is thoroughly wet. If you leave the jar open, you will need to water the soil regularly, but if you close the lid, the humidity inside the jar should provide enough moisture for the plants.

4. Plant the jar

Use the long-handled spoon to excavate small planting holes and lower plants into position. Firm the soil around the rootballs with the spoon. When you have finished planting, drop in some more clay pellets to fill any bare patches.

HINTS AND TIPS

• Lots of green plants will thrive in a bottle garden. Choose tiny specimens of creeping fig, parlor palm, prayer plant, creeping Jenny, polka dot plant, and mind-your-own-business. Avoid succulents, cacti, and plants grown for flowers.

• If you are growing plants in a jar with the lid closed, the glass may occasionally become condensed and cloudy, so open the lid for a few minutes until it clears.

salad patch

A good way to start gardening is with a patch of garden where you can create a bed of favorite salad vegetables and flowers. Include a bamboo teepee to provide support for climbing beans or peas. You don't need much space—a yard-square (metre-square) plot will do. It's a good idea to create a planting pattern on paper before you plant in the soil.

2. Tread down soil
Wearing a pair of boots or sturdy shoes, walk up and down all over the entire bed, putting all your weight on your heels so you push down and compact the soil. This means there will be no uneven lumps or bumps in the bed.

3. Break up lumps
Rake the compacted soil back and forth, so there are no big clods or lumps of soil and the surface is nice and smooth. Remove any big stones that have worked their way to the surface.

1. Spread manure
To give your plants a boost, spread manure all over the soil evenly and lightly dig it in with a spade or fork. It's important to remember to always wear gloves when you handle manure. Now roughly level the surface with a rake.

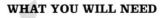

WHAT YOU WILL NEED

- well-rotted manure
- gloves
- spade/fork
- wellies
- rake
- 5 x garden stakes
- garden twine
- hand trowel
- watering can

plants:
- 5 x pole beans
- 4 x tomato (tumbling variety)
- 4 x corn
- 1 x chard
- 1 x zucchini
- 1 x nasturtium
- 1 x lettuce
- 16 x French marigolds

4. Push in stakes

Make a bamboo teepee at the center of the bed. Evenly space five stakes in a circle and push them firmly into the soil, to a depth of about 4 inches (10 cm). You might have to ask a grown-up to help, as it can be hard to push in the stakes.

5. Make teepee

Gather the tops of the stakes together in your hand, cut a long length of garden twine, and then bind the stakes together to finish your teepee. Unless you are very tall, you'll probably need to ask a grown-up to help with this, as well!

6. Plant beans

Dig a hole with a trowel and carefully plant one bean seedling at the base of each stake. Wind the long shoot all the way around the stake, to help it start to climb (if necessary, you can keep it in place with a loosely tied piece of twine).

7. Water seedlings

Newly planted seedlings can wilt very quickly, so remember always to water them straight after planting. Use a watering can with a narrow spout and water the plants directly above the root area, so they get a really good soaking.

8. Add tomatoes

Once you've planted the beans, plant your tomatoes, putting one in the middle of each side of the bed. Dig a hole a few inches (10 cm) from the edge of the bed, and plant a tomato. Repeat for the three remaining sides.

58   growing

9. Plant corn

Excavate a hole at each corner of the bed and plant corn, making sure the roots are well covered with soil. Water well and repeat for each corner.

HINTS AND TIPS

• Slugs and snails will greedily munch their way through salad crops. You can hunt them down by regularly checking the undersides of leaves and removing them.

• You don't have to follow our plan exactly. Colorful lettuces, arugula, eggplant, scallions, carrots, and radish are all easy to grow, while peas can be trained up shorter teepees.

• Apart from adding lots of color to a bed, many flowers, such as nasturtium, calendula (pot marigold), and viola, are edible and can be added to salads, while French marigolds are useful to attract pesky whiteflies away from more precious (and tasty!) plants.

10. Finishing

Use the chard, zucchini, nasturtium, and lettuce plants to fill the gaps left between the corn and the teepee. Now plant the marigolds at even intervals around the edges of the bed. Finish by giving everything a good watering.

carnivorous garden

Watching the jaws of a Venus flytrap snap shut is fascinating, and it's just one of many insect-eating plants you can grow. They come from tropical climates, but are happy outdoors during the summer.

1. Paint pot
Undercoat the pot and let it dry, before adding a light green overcoat. Use a sponge roller to add patches to create a jungly camouflage effect. Leave to dry.

2. Fill with soil
Cover the drainage hole with a stone to stop it from clogging up. Fill the pot with soil, leaving an inch (2.5 cm) between the surface of the soil and the lip of the pot.

5. Water plants
Place the planted-up pot on a large saucer. Now, fill a narrow-spout watering can with rainwater and carefully wet the soil, allowing it to be soaked up before adding more. Stop when the water trickles through the soil and appears in the saucer.

3. Arrange plants
With your plants still in their pots, arrange them on the surface of the soil to create an attractive display.

4. Plant
Use a trowel to dig holes. Each plant's rootball must sit at the same level as the soil. Firm gently with your fingertips.

making

painted pots

These plain terracotta plant pots have been painted in fun bright colors and decorated with bold contrasting spots. Use them indoors or out, or give them as gifts to friends and relatives.

WHAT YOU WILL NEED
- terracotta plant pots
- saucer for paint
- assorted paintbrushes
- undercoat
- colored paint
- pencil
- water-based acrylic varnish

1. Choose materials
Apply undercoat to the pots and let them dry thoroughly. Paint the inside of the pot with the undercoat to about half way down, so that the terracotta does not show. Apply a further coat if required.

2. Paint base color
Apply the base color of the pot to the outside and inside in the same way as the undercoat, and let it dry completely. If required, apply a further coat of paint and let it dry.

3. Finishing
Use a pencil to draw the dots on the outside of the pot. Apply the contrasting paint, using a fine brush to fill in the dots, and let it dry. Finish the pot with a coat of water-based acrylic varnish.

HINTS AND TIPS
- Broad stripes in contrasting colors also look great painted around pots. Once you have applied the base color, use a pencil and draw them on the pot.

Terracotta flowerpot saucers can be painted to match the pots.
- Use a fine brush to paint vegetable motifs on the pots—red tomatoes, chunky orange carrots, or green beans.

wooden nesting box

Plain wooden nesting boxes can be decorated with popsicle sticks and painted in soft pastel colors to create these fun boxes that will make a pretty addition to any tree or wall in the garden. Hang it in a sheltered spot, at least six feet (2 metres) above the ground.

1. Apply undercoat
Use a large paintbrush to apply undercoat to the nesting box. Let it dry completely. Apply a second coat if necessary.

2. Paint base color
Once the undercoat is dry, use a paintbrush to apply the first coat of green paint to the nesting box. Do not paint over the undercoat on the roof, however. Apply a further coat of green paint, if required, and let it dry thoroughly.

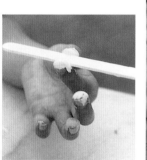

WHAT YOU WILL NEED

- plain wooden nesting box
- undercoat
- paint and paintbrush
- around 6 standard-size wooden popsicle/craft sticks for picket fence
- around 16 large wooden popsicle/craft sticks (depending on size of box) for roof
- strong glue and glue brush
- water-based acrylic varnish

4. Paint sticks for roof

Now take the larger craft sticks and divide them into two. Paint half of the larger sticks green and the other half cream. Let them dry completely. Apply a further coat, if required.

3. Paint popsicle sticks

Apply undercoat to one side and the edges of the standard-sized popsicle sticks, then leave to dry. Paint the other side of the stick and leave to dry. Once completely dry, paint the sticks cream.

wooden nesting box   67

5. Glue on roof

Use strong glue to anchor the large craft sticks to the roof. Glue them in alternate colors to create a striped effect, then leave the glue to dry.

6. Attach picket fence

Ask an adult to cut four of the smaller popsicle sticks in half for the picket fence. Lie them along the base of the front of the nesting box and glue them in an even row along this edge.

HINTS AND TIPS

• Two coats of outdoor varnish will prolong the life of your nesting box. Varnish is available in both water-based and oil-based versions, but if you choose oil-based varnish, it is recommended that an adult applies it, because it's more toxic.

• Try using shades of soft blue paint to create a seaside beach-hut nesting box for a very different, but equally cute, effect.

7. Finishing

Glue the two remaining smaller popsicle sticks horizontally along the top and bottom of the row of popsicle sticks. Finish the nesting box with one or two coats of varnish to make it suitable for outdoor use.

pine cone animals

These cute animals are made from pine cones and are decorated with felt ears, pompom eyes, and pipe-cleaner tails. Different-sized pine cones will lend themselves to different creatures!

1. Draw ear shape
Draw an ear shape on paper and cut out with scissors to make a template. Place the template on the felt and draw around it. Repeat for the second ear.

2. Cut and glue ears
Carefully cut out the ears. Pinch each one in half and put a dab of glue inside the fold to form a pleat. Let it dry completely.

3. Make tail
Cut a length of pipe cleaner approximately 4 inches (10 cm) long and loosely wind it around a finger to create a tail.

4. Glue on tail
Apply a dab of glue to the base of the pine cone and attach the tail to it. Press down gently to make sure the tail is securely in position, and leave to dry completely.

5. Attach ears

Put a small dab of glue on the base of the ears and push them in place between the layers of the pine cone. Use two miniature pompoms for the eyes and glue them just below the ears to finish.

HINTS AND TIPS

• Use one large and one small pine cone to create this mother owl and her baby (left). Cut the wings from felt and use glue to attach them, and a triangle of red felt for the beak, to the sides of the cone. Use pipe cleaners to make the feet.

• Pine cones can also be used to make great Christmas decorations. Paint or spray them gold and silver, then attach loops or ribbon to hang them from.

pine cone animals   71

pressing flowers

Delicate flowers such as pansies and daisies are perfect for pressing, and can be used to make pretty handmade tags or greeting cards to accompany gifts from the garden.

2. Remove flowers
After two or three weeks, carefully remove the flowers from the press. Pressed flowers are very delicate, so lay them on tissue paper to avoid damaging them.

1. Put flowers in press
Carefully position the flowers on the blotting paper provided with a flower press. Leave a gap between each flower or leaf. Screw the press together and leave for two to three weeks in a warm, dry place.

HINTS AND TIPS
- Pick your flowers on a warm, dry day, as wet flowers will go mushy when you press them.
- Dried flowers can be used to make many gifts, such as greetings cards and bookmarks. For a longer-lasting gift, apply a coat of water-based varnish to the item.

3. Apply glue
Carefully apply tiny dabs of glue to the back of the flower or, if preferred, use a very fine paintbrush to apply the glue.

4. Finish off
Turn the flower to the right side and position it on the gift tag. Using your fingertips, carefully press the flower flat and let the glue dry completely.

pebble birdbath

This fun birdbath is made using a broad, shallow terracotta pot saucer and a selection of natural polished pebbles. The birdbath is finished by using grout to fill in the gaps. Place it on a low wall or garden table and watch the birds splashing around!

⭐ **WHAT YOU WILL NEED**
- paintbrush
- gray masonry paint
- terracotta pot saucer approx. 14 inches (35 cm) in diameter
- selection of polished pebbles in assorted colors
- wooden craft stick to apply grout
- waterproof grout and adhesive

1. Paint saucer

Using a thick paintbrush, paint the whole outside and the inside rim of the saucer, and let it dry thoroughly. Apply a further coat of paint if better coverage is required, and leave to dry.

2. Work out design

Arrange the pebbles on the base of the saucer in the required design. Take time to work out your pattern. We chose a flower shape for the center of the plate and arranged the rest of the pebbles in the remaining space.

3. Apply glue

Using the end of a large wooden craft stick, apply a dab of waterproof adhesive and grout to the base of a pebble. Place the pebble on the saucer in your chosen position. Press the pebble gently in place, without using too much pressure.

5. Apply grout

Once the pebbles are firmly in place, use a craft stick to smooth the adhesive and grout over the pebbles and the entire base of the saucer. Now use a damp sponge to smooth the surface of the grout and wipe as much grout as possible from the tops of the pebbles. As the grout dries, remove excess grout with a damp sponge. When almost dry, use a damp sponge to wipe the surface, and when completely dry, use a cloth to polish the pebbles and remove any grout dust.

4. Glue on pebbles

Continue to add the pebbles to the saucer using the waterproof adhesive and grout. When you have completed your pebble design, leave the birdbath to dry completely, preferably overnight.

HINTS AND TIPS
- For a more colorful version of this birdbath, try using the colored glass nuggets that are sometimes used in flower arrangements. Find them at florists and in gift shops.
- Older children can have fun making crazy-paving-effect mosaic designs from pieces of broken china. Make sure that an adult breaks up any plates, as broken pottery has sharp edges that can cut little fingers.

fairy posies and daisy chains

This traditional garden activity will delight little girls of all ages. Miniature posies can be made for dolls or as gifts, while daisy chains make pretty necklaces and wreaths.

WHAT YOU WILL NEED
• tiny assorted flowers
• medium-sized leaf
• scissors
• raffia for ribbon bow

for the daisy chain and caterpillar:
• daisies
• scissors

1. Gather flowers
Pick an assortment of tiny flowers, such as daisies, from the yard and a medium-sized plain leaf in which to wrap them.

2. Arrange posy
Arrange the flowers on the leaf, and fold the leaf around the stems of the flowers to hold them in place. Cut a length of raffia to secure the posy.

3. Finishing
Wrap the length of raffia around the base of the leaf and tie in a neat bow. Trim the ends of the raffia with scissors.

HINTS AND TIPS
• These miniature posies can also be dried to create longer-lasting arrangements. Hang the posy upside down in a warm, dry place for two to three weeks.
• When finishing the pretty floral posies, you could use a length of silk ribbon in a coordinated shade for a more colorful alternative to the raffia. If you are having a tea party, why not put one tiny posy at each place, along with a name card!

1. Collect daisies for chain

Pick a selection of fresh daisies. Break the stems or snip them with scissors, so all the stems are of equal length.

2. Thread daisies

With a fingernail, make a small slit halfway down the stem of the daisy and push another daisy stem through. Repeat until you have the required length of daisy chain.

1. Prepare flower heads

Reserve one main daisy with a long, sturdy stem. Now take another daisy and pinch off the base to leave a hole in the center. Thread this daisy over the main daisy's stem.

2. Finish the caterpillar

Continue to thread daisy heads onto the stem of the main daisy. You will need ten to twelve daisies to make a daisy caterpillar, as shown above.

elf house

This enchanting elf house will delight children of all ages. We used tiny twigs to make furniture and create a magical setting in the shelter of a tree, and added tiny people made of felt.

WHAT YOU WILL NEED
- selection of twigs and bits of bark
- strong glue
- scissors
- felt
- 2 small pompoms
- pipe cleaner
- string for ladder

1. Make the chair

Cut ten 1-inch (2.5 cm) twig lengths and two 2-inch (4 cm) twig lengths for the chair. Glue four shorter lengths together with one short length along the back for the seat. Glue two twigs to the front corners of the seat for legs. Glue the two longer twigs to a shorter length to form a chair back. Add a shorter twig to the center as a support.

2. Glue together
Apply a dab of glue to the back corners of the base of the chair and stick to the back of the chair. Hold the chair together as the glue dries.

3. Make table
Take a small oval-shaped piece of bark and cut four 1-inch (2.5 cm) twigs for the legs. Apply a dab of glue to the top of each twig and attach to the bottom of the bark about ¾ inch (2 cm) apart. Let the glue dry thoroughly.

4. Cut out felt people
Cut a quarter-circle of felt 1½ inches (3 cm) in diameter. Roll into a cone so the straight edges overlap by ⅛ inch (2 mm) and glue along this line. Apply a dab of glue to the pompom and stick to the top of the cone.

5. Make arms
Cut one 2¼-inch (5-cm) length of pipe cleaner and wrap it once around the top of the cone to form the arms.

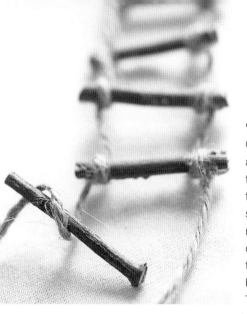

7. Finishing the ladder

Glue the next twig to the string approximately ¾ inch (2 cm) from the first and twist the string around the twig. Repeat to form the first side of the ladder. Using the same method, glue on the second length of the string on the other side of the ladder, making sure the spaces between each twig are the same. Trim the ends of the string to finish.

6. Cut twigs for ladder

To make the ladder, cut six 1½-inch (3-cm) twig lengths and two 8-inch (20-cm) pieces of string. Apply a dab of glue to the end of the first twig and attach the end of the string, wrapping the string around the twig as you do so. Hold the string and twig together as the glue dries.

HINTS AND TIPS

• Use longer lengths of twig to make a larger platform on which to place the people and furniture.

• Tiny acorn cups make great bowls for the table!

• If you wish to leave the elf house outdoors permanently, apply a coat or two of exterior varnish to the platform and furniture to make it more durable.

burlap tote

Use natural burlap to make this practical yet pretty garden tote and use it to hold garden tools, seeds, plant labels, and other gardening essentials. With its simple painted design of peas and carrots, it would make a great gift, too.

1. Cut out fabric

Take the length of burlap and cut a piece measuring 7 x 22 inches (18 x 55 cm) for the bag, four 4-inch (10-cm) squares for the pockets, one oval with a diameter of 5 x 8 inches (14 x 21 cm) for the base, and two lengths measuring 3 x 10 inches (8 x 24 cm) for the handles. Use the selvage of the fabric for the top of the pockets and for one longer side of the handle sections to prevent fraying.

2. Decorate pockets

On the remaining three edges of each pocket, pull away strands of burlap to fray the edges about ½ inch (1 cm) from each side. Use a brush to paint a design on the pockets. Set the paint according to the manufacturer's directions.

3. Attach pockets

On the length of the large burlap rectangle, allowing ½ inch (1 cm) at each end for the seams, pin the pockets in place at evenly spaced intervals. Using green embroidery thread, make small running stitches to attach the pockets to the bag, leaving the selvage edge open at the top.

- 12 inches (30 cm) burlap fabric (approx. 52 inches (137 cm) wide)
- scissors
- fabric paint in green and orange
- fine paintbrush
- lime green and brown embroidery thread
- needle
- pins
- iron-on fusible interlining

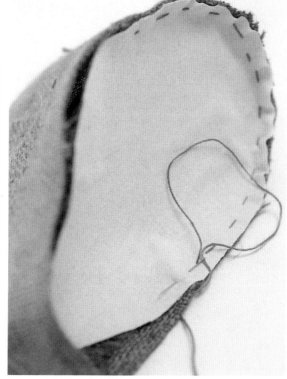

4. Sew seam

Fold the large piece of burlap with right sides together, and stitch the sides of the bag together ½ inch (1 cm) from the edge. Turn right side out and press both layers of the seam to one side. Using brown embroidery thread, stitch a row of running stitches along this seam to prevent it from fraying.

5. Stitch base to bag

Iron the fusible interlining to one side of the burlap oval (it is advisable for an adult to do this). Now, with right sides together, stitch the oval to the bag. Whipstitch around the raw edges to prevent fraying.

6. Stitch top hem

Turn the top of the bag 1½ inches (3 cm) to the inside and press with an iron. Use lime green embroidery thread and running stitch to secure in place.

7. Make handles

Lie the two handle sections flat, turn the top and bottom over by ½ inch (1 cm) and press. Fold the long edges ¾ inch (2 cm) to the inside, with the selvage on top. Use running stitch to hold in place.

HINTS AND TIPS

• Try painting different garden motifs such as leaves or trees on the pockets, or paint on the child's initials or name.
• You could make a tote from brightly colored felt for a younger child. Cut the felt with pinking shears and the edges will not fray. Jazz up the tote by appliqueing it with leaf and flower motifs

8. Finishing

Stitch the ends of the handles to the inside of the bag approximately 5 inches (12 cm) apart. The handles are positioned along the sides of the oval base shape, just above the pockets. Use whipstitch to hold the handles in position.

lavender bags

These simple lavender bags are easy to sew and make lovely gifts for family and friends. Use a combination of pastel-colored floral and dotted cotton fabrics for pretty vintage-style lavender bags.

WHAT YOU WILL NEED
- lavender
- floral fabric. Each bag uses two rectangles of fabric approx. 5 x 8 inches (12 x 20 cm) or a single rectangle 5 x 16 inches (12 x 40 cm)
- pinking shears
- scissors
- cotton embroidery thread
- needle
- 10 inches narrow white cotton ribbon per bag

2. Cut out the bags

Using pinking shears, cut out a rectangle of fabric measuring 5 x 16 inches (12 x 40 cm), or two rectangles each measuring 5 x 8 inches (12 x 20 cm).

1. Cut and dry lavender

Using scissors, carefully snip off long stems of lavender. Cover a tray with a sheet of waxed paper and place the lavender on top to dry. Put the tray in a warm, dry place until the herbs have dried completely. When dry, carefully pull off the lavender heads by hand and collect them in a bowl ready to fill your bags.

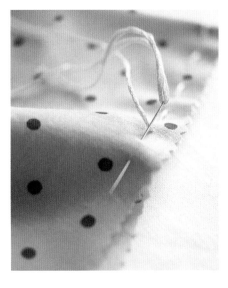

3. Stitch bags

With wrong sides together, stitch together the sides of the fabric and base of bag using running stitch and contrasting cotton embroidery thread. The stitches should be no more than ½ inch (1 cm) apart, so the lavender does not leak out.

5. Finishing

Lay the bag on one side and wrap the cotton ribbon around the bag just above the lavender. Tie a bow and trim the ends using scissors.

4. Fill with lavender

When the bag is complete, carefully fill it with loose lavender using a teaspoon. Fill the bag approximately halfway up, but make sure it is plump and full.

HINTS AND TIPS

• Look out for pretty dresses or skirts in thrift stores, which can be cut up to use for lavender bags.

• Felt hearts cut with pinking shears can also be filled with lavender. Stitch on fabric loops to make hanging lavender bags.

• Dried rose petals make an equally fragrant filler for these pretty bags. Dry them, then crush the petals gently and fill the bags, before tying with ribbon bows.

printed apron

This fun gardening apron is printed with a design of apples, created using the traditional potato-printing method. The familiar outline of the apple makes a simple, bold motif on the fabric when printed. You can use a purchased apron or, if you like sewing, you can make your own from muslin and colorful bias binding.

WHAT YOU WILL NEED
* apple
* sharp knife for cutting apple
* kitchen paper
* fabric paint
* saucer for paint
* small sponge paint roller
* plain cotton apron

1. Apply paint to stamp
Ask a grown-up to cut the apple in half. Blot it with paper towel to remove excess moisture. Squirt some paint in a saucer, dip the paint roller in the paint, and blot on side of plate to remove excess paint. Apply paint to the apple.

2. Stamp design on apron
Carefully place the apple cut-side down on the apron and press down firmly to make the imprint. Use a slight rocking motion to make sure the paint has been applied to the whole area, but be careful not to smudge it.

3. Finishing
Using the roller, apply more paint to the apple, then repeat the design all the way around the apron, as desired. Let the paint dry thoroughly, then iron the apron to seal the paint (following the manufacturer's directions).

HINTS AND TIPS
* Try cutting different fruits and vegetables such as broccoli, carrots, and cauliflower in half—they will all create interesting veggie motifs on fabric.

* This traditional printing method is fun and easy, and works just as well on cards and paper as on fabric—see the potato-print wrapping paper and cards project on pages 94–95, for example.

tin-can wind chime

Make a musical wind chime using an old tin can and pretty glass beads to catch the light, then hang it from a tree in the yard. The tin is pierced with small holes for the hanging decorations. Ask an adult to do this before getting started on the project.

1. Pierce holes

Ask an adult to pierce the holes in the tin can before you start. You need two holes on each side of the open end of the can for the hanging wire. On the bottom of the can, pierce one hole in the center, four holes evenly spaced around the outside edge, and four holes evenly spaced around the central hole. Now use a fine paintbrush to paint four narrow stripes around the outside of the can, using the ridges of the can as an outline.

2. Start threading

Cut a length of string approximately 8 inches (20 cm) long and attach one of the metal bells to the bottom, knotting it several times to secure. Begin threading four glass beads onto the string.

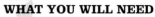

WHAT YOU WILL NEED
- Clean tin can with one end removed
- awl for punching holes
- Fine paintbrush
- Acrylic paint for stripes
- thin string
- scissors
- 5 small jingle bells
- 20 large glass beads
- 9 small beads
- 1 metal clapper
- four tubular chimes
- 12 inches (30 cm) fine wire

4. Thread on clapper

Take a length of string approximately 8 inches (20 cm) long and attach a bell to the end. Knot in place. Thread on the metal clapper, so that it hangs from the bottom of the thread, just above the bell.

5. Thread on chimes

Cut a piece of thread approximately 12 inches (30 cm) long. Double it, and knot the ends. Now thread it through the hole in the tubular chime and pull through so it forms a loop.

3. Tie on bells

Repeat until you have made four bead lengths. We used colored glass beads, but you could use varnished wood beads for a more natural effect.

• Both wooden and metal wind-chime kits can be found in craft stores or on the internet, allowing you to add your own decorations to finish.
• Alternatively, you could take an old wind chime to pieces and reuse the different parts, along with some pretty new beads and bells, to create our tin-can wind chime.

6. Tie on thread

The tubular chimes, clapper, and beaded decorations are all attached to the inside of the tin by feeding the strings through the holes in the can's base and pulling through. The clapper must go through the central hole in the bottom of the tin and the tubular chimes around this. Finally, thread the beaded decorations through the outside holes.

7. Fix wire handle

Thread the 12-inch (30 cm) length of wire through the two holes in the sides of the top (open) end of the can. Twist the wire around itself to secure in place. This is the loop from which to hang your wind chime.

8. Finishing

Gather all the pieces of string together, push the ends through a bead, and knot securely. The bead will prevent the string from slipping through the hole in the base.

pretty seed packets

It's fun and satisfying harvesting your own seeds and then packaging them for the following year in these pretty decorated envelopes. You could also give them to family and friends.

WHAT YOU WILL NEED
- small brown envelopes
- colored pencils
- hole punch
- seeds
- approximately 10 inches (25 cm) raffia ribbon per envelope
- scissors

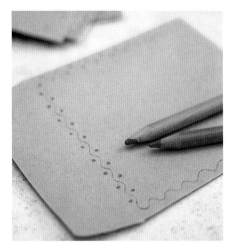

1. Decorate envelope
Decorate the edges of the front of the envelope with pretty designs such as wavy lines and and tiny polka dots.

2. Draw on design
Now draw the shape of a flower or vegetable, depending on what seeds are in the envelope, and fill in the design using the coloring pencils. You might like to add the name of the seeds in your best handwriting.

3. Punch holes
Use a hole punch to make two holes at the top of the envelope, just where the flap is situated. Now carefully put the seeds in the envelope, and seal it closed.

4. Finishing

Thread the raffia through the two punched holes and tie in a decorative bow. Trim the ends of the raffia with scissors to finish.

HINTS AND TIPS

• Wrap tiny seeds in a piece of tissue paper and seal with tape before placing in the envelope.

• These envelopes would also look great decorated with potato-print designs—see pages 94–95.

• Look up on the internet the Latin names for the plants and write them on the front in your very best handwriting!

potato printing

Homegrown potatoes are not only delicious to eat, but can also be used for fun craft projects such as printing. You can even make your own wrapping paper and greeting cards by using a cut potato to stamp on a simple leaf-shaped design.

WHAT YOU WILL NEED
• medium-sized potato
• kitchen paper
• paint
• paintbrush
• brown wrapping paper
• card label for gift tag

1. Cut design
Ask an adult to cut the potato in half and carve out the leaf shape. Blot the potato with a paper towel to remove excess moisture. Apply paint to the leaf motif using a paintbrush.

2. Print pattern
Carefully press the potato onto the paper to print the leaf design. Use a slight rocking motion to make sure that all the paint has been applied to the whole area.

3. Finish off
Repeat the design all over the paper at regular spacings, and let the paper dry thoroughly. Print a single leaf motif on greeting cards and gift tags to coordinate with your pretty wrapping paper.

HINTS AND TIPS
• Potato printing works equally well on fabric using fabric paints—see our printed apron on pages 86–87, which would look great in a potato print, too.

• Using a cookie cutter, make a star shape on the potato, then use this stamp to make your own Christmas wrapping paper and cards. Try using festive red paint on white paper.

bird feeder

Attract wild birds to your garden with this fun bird feeder. We made it from a pumpkin, which was then decorated with cloves and filled with a generous heap of birdseed. Hang it from a tree in your yard and watch the birds tuck in!

WHAT YOU WILL NEED
- small pumpkin
- awl (for piercing holes in pumpkin)
- dried cloves
- scissors
- string
- small nail
- 1 packet suet
- saucepan
- birdseed mix
- spoon

1. Cut pumpkin in half
Ask an adult to cut the pumpkin in half and scoop out the flesh from the inside (the seeds can be used to make the necklace on pages 100–101). The holes for the cloves are pierced using an awl, so it is advisable for an adult to do this. Insert the cloves around the edge of the pumpkin in two parallel rows.

2. Plait string
Cut six 3-foot (1-m) long pieces of string. Take three strands and knot them together at one end. Start plaiting the string (it may be easier if someone helps you by holding the knotted end). When the first length is finished, plait the remaining three lengths to form the second hanging loop.

3. Attach hanging loops
Turn the pumpkin upside down. Lay the plaited string in an X across the base. Ask an adult to push in a nail to hold the string in place.

4. Finishing

Melt the suet in a saucepan until it becomes liquid. Add the birdseed and stir until the mixture becomes firm. Carefully spoon the mixture into the squash bowl. Tie the ends of the string around a branch of a tree, and trim the ends using scissors.

HINTS AND TIPS

• For a more permanent bird feeder, use a small wooden bowl and ask an adult to drill four holes just below the rim. Suspend from plaited string hanging loops, and fill with the seed and suet mix.

• Use the birdseed mix to fill nylon net bags that peanuts or garlic are sold in. Pour in the seed mix and hang from a tree in the yard.

peanut heart

Unshelled peanuts can be pierced and threaded on wire to create bird feeders that our feathered friends will appreciate in the winter months. We finished the feeder with a raffia bow to create a pretty and practical garden ornament.

WHAT YOU WILL NEED
- unshelled peanuts
- wooden skewer or awl for piercing holes
- strong wire
- raffia for bow
- approx. 8 inches (20 cm) twine for hanging loop

1. Pierce holes in peanuts
Ask an adult to pierce the holes in the nuts using a wooden skewer or an awl. You will need approximately 60 peanuts for one peanut heart.

HINTS AND TIPS
- It is recommended that an adult pierces the holes in the peanuts, as both awls and skewers are sharp.
- For variety, try experimenting with different wire shapes, such as circles and ovals. Both would make ideal bird feeders.
- This peanut heart makes a great gift for any bird-loving relatives!

2. Thread peanuts
Fold the wire in half to create the V shape of the base of the heart. Begin threading peanuts onto the wire. Each side needs around 30 peanuts.

3. Finishing
Ask an adult to bend each side of the heart into a curve to form a heart shape and twist the wire to anchor the ends in place. Now tie a raffia bow at the top of the heart to cover the wire ends. Cut an 8-inch (20-cm) length of twine to make a hanging loop, and hang the feeder from a tree branch.

seed necklace

When it's too cold or wet to play outside, why not make your own jewelry from dried pumpkin seeds and sycamore wings threaded on fine string? It's a great way of using up the seeds from the carved Halloween pumpkin project on pages 102–103.

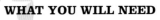

WHAT YOU WILL NEED
- spoon
- pumpkin seeds
- bowl of warm water
- colander
- tray
- dishcloth
- needle for making holes
- fine string
- sycamore wings

1. Remove seeds
Using a spoon, loosen the pumpkin flesh, then scoop out the flesh and seeds from the pumpkin with your hands.

2. Wash them
Put all the seeds in a bowl of warm water and leave them to soak for a couple of hours so the flesh comes away from the seeds. Carefully pick out the seeds and place in a colander.

3. Rinse seeds
When all the seeds are in the colander, put it under running water to remove any remaining vestiges of pumpkin flesh.

4. Dry seeds
Lay out the seeds in rows on a tray covered with a clean dishcloth. Leave in a warm dry place until the seeds have dried out. This can take up to a week.

4. Pierce holes

When the seeds are dry, use a needle to pierce holes through each seed ready for threading onto the necklace. It is advisable for an adult to carry out this task for younger children.

5. Thread on seeds

Thread the string on the needle and knot the ends. Begin threading the seeds and intersperse them with sycamore wings. When threading is complete, tie the ends of the thread in a knot to finish.

HINTS AND TIPS

• To create matching bracelets, cut shorter lengths of fine elastic and thread on the pumpkin seeds then knot the ends. These make great party favors!

• Paint the pumpkin seeds in a variety of pretty colors after they have been dried.

• Intersperse small wooden beads in colored or natural finishes with the seeds for a more decorative necklace.

jack o' lantern

This carved Halloween pumpkin looks more friendly than spooky! He's been given a pointy parsnip nose and a thick head of carrot-frond hair. Fill him with votive candles and leave him by the door to greet trick-or-treaters, or use him as a table centerpiece.

WHAT YOU WILL NEED
• large pumpkin
• sharp knife
• ice-cream scoop or spoon for scooping
• felt-tip pen
• parsnip for nose
• carrot fronds for hair

1. Scoop out seeds
Ask an adult to cut the top off the pumpkin using a sharp knife. Scoop out the flesh and seeds using an ice-cream scoop or a large spoon.

2. Draw on face
Draw eyes, nose, and a mouth on the pumpkin using a marker pen. Ask an adult to cut out the shapes using a sharp knife.

3. Insert nose
Push the thick end of the parsnip into the nose hole to make a nose. Cut the fronds from the carrots to prepare the hair.

HINTS AND TIPS
• Set aside the pumpkin seeds to make pretty necklaces, as shown on pages 100–101. The seeds will need to be thoroughly washed and dried first.
• The pumpkin flesh can also be used to make delicious pumpkin soup and yummy pumpkin pie to serve at Halloween!

4. Finishing
Lay the carrot fronds around the top of the pumpkin to make the hair. Insert votive candles inside the pumpkin and ask an adult to light them. Now place the pumpkin on a pile of dried leaves by the front door or on the dining table.

scarecrow

Children will love making this friendly scarecrow and dressing it up in an assortment of their old clothes. When placed in the center of the vegetable patch, it will hopefully deter rascally birds from eating their home-grown produce!

1. Make head

To make the scarecrow's head, cut a piece of burlap measuring 16 x 22 inches (40 x 55 cm). With right sides together, fold the fabric in half along the longest edge, then stitch along this edge ¾ inch (2 cm) from the raw edge.

2. Stuff head

Turn the burlap right side out. Tie a piece of string around the top of the burlap and knot tightly. Gently pull strands of the burlap to make a frayed edge. Now stuff the burlap head with straw until it is firm and full.

3. Paint on face

Use a paintbrush to paint the eyes and mouth on the front of the burlap to create the scarecrow's head. Let the paint dry.

WHAT YOU WILL NEED

- burlap for head
- needle
- thread
- ball of string
- straw for filling
- paint for face
- paintbrush
- 2 wooden dowel poles, 4 feet (1.2 m) and 3 feet (1 m) long
- old shirt
- old overalls
- straw hat

4. Make frame

Lay the longer wooden dowel on the ground and place the shorter one across it, approximately 16 inches (40 cm) down from the top, to form a cross shape. Tie a length of string around the cross, wrapping it securely to hold the dowels in place.

5. Anchor frame

Push the dowel into the ground. You may have to dig a hole in the earth and then pat the earth firmly around the base of the dowel. Place the open end of the scarecrow's head over the dowel, and tie the base with string to secure it.

6. Dress scarecrow

Unbutton the shirt and put it on the scarecrow. Tightly tie a length of string around the bottom. This will prevent the straw stuffing from falling out of the shirt.

7. Stuff with straw

Stuff the shirt with straw in the arms and body to pad out the fabric and form the scarecrow shape. Continue to fill the shirt until the body is nice and plump.

HINTS AND TIPS

• An upturned terracotta flowerpot makes a fun head for a scarecrow and can easily be painted with a sassy face. Make sure the hole in the pot is big enough to fit the dowel through.

• Use your own old clothes to dress up your scarecrow, or look for clothes in thrift stores.

• Deter particularly persistent birds by hanging shiny CDs from the end of the scarecrow's arms.

8. Finishing

Place the overalls on the scarecrow (you may find it easier to cut a hole in the seat to thread the dowel through). Now stuff the legs of the overalls with more straw. Place a jaunty straw hat on the scarecrow's head to finish.

harvest wreath

Decorate a ready-made wreath with your own dried leaves to create a decorative harvest wreath to hang on the wall or front door. Collect a variety of attractive, different-colored leaves in the fall and use a flower press or large book to press them flat.

WHAT YOU WILL NEED
- dried leaves
- heart-shaped wreath
- glue
- dried seedheads and sycamore wings
- 10 inches (25 cm) red gingham ribbon

1. Collect and dry leaves
Collect leaves for drying, making sure they are not damp. Place them between layers of paper in a thick book or flower press and leave for two or three weeks until dry. Put a dab of glue on the back of each leaf, and attach to the heart wreath.

2. Glue on leaves
Continue to glue leaves to the wreath and add sycamore wings and dried seedheads at regular intervals. Let the glue dry completely.

3. Finishing
Thread the gingham ribbon through the top of the heart wreath. Then tie in a knot so you have a hanging loop to suspend the wreath.

HINTS AND TIPS

- For a more festive wreath, paint or spray the leaves using gold and silver paint as used for our Christmas wreath (pages 110–111).

- Pretty, brightly colored berries can also be purchased or dried and used for added interest on the harvest wreath, but make absolutely sure they are not of a poisonous variety.

christmas wreath

Delicately shaped dried leaves, nuts, and seedheads are painted silver and gold and used to adorn this stunning Christmas wreath, which will gladden any front door during the festive season.

1. Dry and paint leaves
Gather leaves to dry from the yard or a park. Lay them between layers of paper in a thick book or a flower press and leave for two to three weeks until dry. When dry, paint the leaves gold and silver and let them dry. If necessary, apply a further coat of paint for even coverage.

2. Paint nuts and seedheads
Take the nuts and seedheads and paint them gold and silver using a fine paintbrush. Leave them to dry alongside the painted leaves.

3. Glue on leaf
Apply dabs of glue to the back of a leaf and place it in position on the wreath. Press down gently on the leaf to attach it to the wreath.

4. Attach rest of leaves

Take another leaf and apply glue to the back before sticking it to the wreath. Continue with this process until all the painted leaves are glued to the wreath.

5. Finishing

Add the nuts and seedheads. Wrap the ribbon around the top of the wreath and tie in a bow. To finish, add a length of string to hang the wreath.

HINTS AND TIPS

• It may be easier to use a hot glue gun to attach the seedheads and nuts. It is recommended that an adult uses the glue gun if younger children are working on this project.

• Miniature pine cones look great on Christmas wreaths, too. Paint them silver and gold, just like the seedheads, and stick them on using a hot glue gun.

• For a rustic Scandinavian look, paint the leaves red and white.

twig decorations

These delicate-looking star decorations are made from thin twigs gathered from the yard or the park, painted silver and tied together with fine wire. The twig stars look pretty suspended from a mantelpiece or hung in groups on a Christmas tree.

WHAT YOU WILL NEED
• thin twigs
• silver paint
• fine paintbrush
• fine wire for tying
• scissors
• silver cotton or nylon thread for hanging loops

1. Apply paint
Choose three 4-inch (10-cm) twigs and paint them silver. Leave to dry thoroughly. If required, apply a second coat of paint for even coverage and leave to dry.

2. Form star shape
Lay the three twigs one on top of each other to form a star shape. Cut a length of fine wire and bind it around the twigs to hold the star in place. Wrap the wire over the twigs several times so they are completely secure.

3. Attach hanging loop
Cut a length of thread for the hanging loop and fold in half. Wrap it around one "arm" of the star, thread the ends back through the loop, and pull to attach the thread to the twig. Knot the two loose ends together to form a hanging loop.

HINTS AND TIPS
• Try painting the twig stars red and white and suspending the decorations from branches in a large vase for a pretty and festive table display.

• Once the twigs have been painted, apply a thin line of glue along each twig, hold them over a plate or piece of newspaper, and sprinkle with gold or silver glitter for sparkly decorations.

outdoor fun

treasure hunts

A garden full of towering trees, shrubs, or leafy exotics, with narrow paths cut through the display of plants, makes an exciting place for scavenger hunts or to follow clues that lead to a hidden treasure trove!

Scavenger hunts

Kids love scavenger hunts—they're lots of fun and very easy to set up. All you need to do is spend a few minutes walking around the garden and putting together a list of objects that you can challenge the children to find. Although this is an ideal game to play at parties or to keep groups of kids entertained during school vacations, it can also be played by a child alone. Pine cones, fruit, feathers, shells, colored pebbles, and flowers are all perfect for the list, but be creative and add some more unusual items. Older kids may enjoy the extra competitive element of a time limit.

Treasure hunts

A treasure hunt would be a complete disappointment without an exciting treasure trove to uncover, so fill a small chest or box with foil-wrapped chocolate coins, marbles, or other treats that your kids love. Stow it out of sight, then put together a list of numbered clues that the kids have to solve and which will lead them to the treasure! Mark the numbers on tags, leaf-shaped bits of paper, or rolled-up sheets of paper, and write the clues to the next number on the back. Hang clues from the lower branches of a tree, tuck them into gaps in the wall, or hide them under pots. You can even have themed treasure hunts at special times of the year, such as an Easter egg hunt.

Plant bingo

This is a great way for your kids to learn about leaves. Put together a small grid on a sheet of paper and, in every square, draw the shape of a different leaf that can be found in your garden. Each leaf can be crossed out as it's found, and the first child to complete the grid is the winner.

garden games

While television, games systems, and computers all have their place, encouraging children to play traditional games outdoors is good for their health and helps them to appreciate that the garden is not somewhere simply to grow plants, but somewhere they can have fun with their friends.

Fun and games

There are lots of games kids can play, whatever the size of your yard. If you live in an apartment or have a tiny yard, there's no excuse—a public park is a perfect place for kids to burn off energy.

Traditional games

Young children love to play scary games, such as "What's the time, Mr. Wolf?". Ask kids to draw straws or flip a coin to decide who will be Mr. Wolf first. Mr. Wolf stands at one end of the yard and turns his back on the rest of the group. Line the other children up at the opposite end of the yard. They shout, "What's the time, Mr. Wolf?". The Wolf replies by saying "One o'clock" or "Nine o'clock," and so on, and the children take a step forward. When the Wolf says "Dinner time," the kids run as the Wolf

chases them. The child that is tagged then takes a turn at being the Wolf.

"Grandmother's Footsteps" is a variation on the "Mr. Wolf" theme. All the children try to creep up on Grandmother, who can turn around at any moment. When she does, the players must freeze. Anyone seen moving is sent back to the start line. The first child to reach Grandmother takes her place.

Letting off steam

Large yards are perfect for ball games, races, and chase games, such as tag, "Stuck in the Mud," and "Kick the Can," but smaller spaces also have plenty of potential for fun. Hopscotch doesn't take up much space, while jumping rope, Chinese jump rope, or blowing big bubbles with soapy water can all be done in a yard the size of a hankerchief!

water play

There's no better way of cooling down on a long, hot summer's day than splashing in water. There are lots of wet-play activies your kids can get stuck into, such as messing around with water pistols or racing boats in a wading pool, but with a little bit of imagination you could invent some games of your own.

Car wash

On a sunny day, show the kids how to set up their very own backyard car wash. Wheel out their bikes, tricycles, or scooters from the garage or garden shed, and line them up in a row. Now show your kids how to hose them down, using a bowl of soapy water and a scrubbing brush to remove any stubborn patches of dirt. If the children have plastic toys or a tea set, these can be swished around in a plastic bowl and left to dry in the sun.

Water painting

Budding artists will enjoy getting stuck into water painting on a dry patio or path. It's easy, doesn't call for any special equipment and won't leave marks that are hard to clean off. All the kids need is a bowl of water and a paintbrush. Dip the brush into the water and encourage them to paint funny faces, strange creatures, or pretty patterns. Alternatively, you could fill an empty liquid detergent bottle with water and your kids can squirt their name or a message onto the ground. If you have colored chalks, let the kids get to work on their very own masterpieces, then have lots of fun washing them off later with a big bowl of soapy water.

Water tag

When friends come over, encourage the kids to let off steam by having a water fight or by playing water tag. All you need to do is soak a sponge in water and decide who's going to be "it." In turn, whoever they hit with the wet sponge becomes "it." So what are you waiting for? Grab a towel, put their swimsuits on, and let the fun begin!

mini-beasts

If they carefully move stones, look under pieces of rotting wood, or dig a shallow hole in the soil, children are likely to spot a mini-beast or two taking shelter or scavenging for food.

A backyard safari

Whether you live in the countryside or in the heart of the city, have rolling acres or a small plot, your yard will still be full of tiny creatures that can be tracked down by taking kids on a backyard safari.

Some of these creatures will be instantly recognizable, such as slugs, snails, spiders, earthworms, ladybugs, bees, and butterflies. Others are less well known, and every area of the country has types that are common there. This miniature insect kingdom is fascinating for children to explore, and if they look carefully they are sure to find many different creatures in a matter of minutes.

Intrepid explorers

Although kids can head outdoors and start searching immediately, it's fun to put together an explorers' kit first. It is easy to do and will help them remember everything they

have seen. All they need is a magnifying glass, a notebook, and a pen or pencil to record what they have seen. If they enjoy drawing, children could try to sketch the different mini-beasts they find. And as their spotting skills develop, why not add a cheap digital camera to their kit? Kids will enjoy taking snaps of fast-moving or shy creatures, such as butterflies, which can later be downloaded onto a computer, identified from the photo, then stuck into a special mini-beasts scrapbook.

Identifying the beasts

There are many commonly found mini-beasts that are easy to identify, but children may discover a more unusual creature. A good book on garden wildlife, either purchased or borrowed from the library, will help enormously when it comes to identifying the many different mini-beasts you've tracked down.

suppliers

Garden tools and equipment

Arizona Pottery
1-800-420-1808
www.arizonapottery.com
Terracotta pottery, including pots
in many different shapes and
sizes, both with drain holes and
without. Also strawberry planters,
troughs, urns, bowls, and
saucers.

Brooks Barrel Company
800-398-2766
www.brooksbarrel.com
Handcrafted wooden barrels,
kegs and planters of all sizes.
Good for growing seed potatoes.

Gardener's Supply Company
128 Intervale Road
Burlington, VT 05401
802-660-3505
Call 1-888-833-1412 or visit
www.gardeners.com
Everything for the garden, from
tools to pottery to fertilizers and
soil to plant markers. Also a
selection of birding products that
will attract wildlife to the garden.

Home Depot
www.homedepot.com
Visit one of their 1500 stores
across North America for garden
tools and equipment, potting
mixes, pottery planters and
saucers, mulches, chippings, and
seeds.

Kinsman Company
River Road
Point Pleasant, PA 18950-0357
800-733-4146
www.kinsmangarden.com
Watering cans in bright colors
and hanging baskets with liners.

Lowe's Home Centers
Call (800) 445-6937 or visit
www.lowes.com for details of
your nearest store.
Soil, sand, potting mix, mulches,
chippings, flower and plant foods,
insect control chemicals,
fertilizers, and garden tools.

**The National Gardening
Association**
Visit their website especially for
kids at www.kidsgardening.com
Their 'Gardening with Kids' store
www.kidsgardeningstore.com
offers mini wheelbarrows, gloves,
kids' tools, plant markers, a
garden tool organizer and more.

Pottery Barn Kids
Call 800-993-4923 or visit
www.potterybarnkids.com for
details of your nearest store.
Sandboxes and cute garden
furniture for kids.

Smith & Hawken
Call 1-800-940-1170 or visit
www.smithandhawken.com for
details of your nearest store.
Their "Sprouts" line offers cute,
colorful boots, watering cans,
trugs, pint-sized tool kits, and
other essentials for green-
thumbed kids.

Windowbox.com
1-888-GARDEN-Box
www.windowbox.com
Windowboxes, pots, bowls,
saucers, and hanging baskets.
Also a good selection of junior
gardener's equipment.

Crafting equipment

A. C. Moore
Visit www.acmoore.com for
details of your nearest store.
Chain of craft superstores. Visit
their website for some fun craft
projects for kids.

Britex Fabrics
146 Geary Street
San Francisco, CA 94108
415-392-2910
www.britexfabrics.com
Wide variety of pretty ribbons,
trims, and notions that are great
for adding a finishing touch to
wreaths or lavender bags.

Crafting Direct
www.craftingdirect.com
Essential crafting equipment for
kids: cards and papers, white
glue, fabric paints, ready-pressed
flowers, packs of sequins and
beads, and more.

Dick Blick Art Materials
Locations throughout the
Midwest. Visit www.dickblick.com
for details of your nearest store.
Air-drying clay, balsa wood, cold-
water fabric dyes, fabric paint and
stencilling equipment, glue, felt,
and cutting tools.

Discount School Supplies
www.discountschoolsupplies.com
Arts and crafts materials for early
learners. Colored pipe cleaners,
felt, wooden craft sticks, glue,
and ready-made pompoms.

E Burlap
877-885-7527
www.eburlap.com
Burlap rolls, ready-made bags,
and squares, for general garden
tasks as well as the scarecrow
and the garden tote projects.

Hobby Lobby
Locations nationwide.
Call 405-745-1100 or visit
www.hobbylobby.com for details
of your nearest store.
Discount arts and crafts stores.
Find suggestions for kids' crafts
on their website.

House Fabric
314-968-0090
www.housefabric.com
Burlap fabric as well as canvas
and denim, and printed cotton
fabrics that are ideal for the
lavender bags project.

JoAnn Fabrics
Locations nationwide.
Visit www.joann.com for details of
your nearest store.
Art and crafts supplier offering a
wide selection of paper, cards,
craft materials, fabric,
scrapbooking materials, and
more.

Loose Ends
2065 Madrona Ave. SE
Salem, OR 97302
www.looseends.com
Craft materials including dried
flowers and foliage, raffia ribbon,
gift wrap, dried lavender, many
different ribbons and ties, and
much more.

Merrit Lavender Farm
87450 McTimmons Lane
Bandon, OR 97411
541-347-7190
www.lavenderladyfarm.com
Organically grown dried lavender
for lavender bags.

Michaels
Locations nationwide.
Visit www.michaels.com for
details of your nearest store.
A huge selection of every kind of
art and craft material. They have
special areas for kids' products,
including air-drying clay, easy
sewing kits, plain keepsake boxes
to decorate, collage materials,
Makit & Bakit® ceramic painting
kits, and essential basics like glue
and paint.

Paper Source
www.paper-source.com
Simple, stylish crafting kits for
mother's day presents as well as
many other special occasions.
Also envelopes, cards, and pretty
handmade paper in a variety of
designs, as well as crafting basics
such as scissors, glue, and hole
punches.

Paper Wishes
888-300-3406
www.paperwishes.com
Good for card-making
equipment, different kinds of
paper, scrapbooks, stamps and
stamping accessories, stickers,
tools, and more.

Pearl Art and Crafts Supplies
1-800-451-7327
www.pearlpaint.com
Discount art supplier offering
hundreds of different items,
including air-drying clay, ceramic
paint, and sketchbooks for kids.

Prizm
The Artist's Supply Store
5688 Mayfield Rd.
Cleveland, OH 44124
440-605-9434
Visit www.prizmart.com for details
of their other stores.
Paints, paper, clay and ceramics,
markers and pens, and more art
supplies.

Target
Locations nationwide
Visit www.target.com for details
of your nearest store.
A good selection of varied crafting
equipment is available from their
children's toy departments. Craft
kits, clay and pottery supplies,
scrapbooking accessories,
crafting tools, and more.

Utrecht
Stores nationwide.
Visit www.utrechtart.com for
details of your nearest store.
Useful source of discount art and
craft supplies.

Plants

Avant Gardens
710 High Hill Road
North Dartmouth, MA 02747
508-998-8819
www.avantgardensNE.com
Good selection of alpine plants
and succulents. Also colorful
annuals for fun displays.

California Cactus Centre
216 South Rosemead Boulevard
Pasadena, CA 91107
626-795-2788
www.cactuscenter.com
Cacti and succulents.

Daniel's Specialty Nursery
http://danielscactus.hypermart.net
4,000 varieties of cacti and
succulents.

**Irish Eyes – Garden City
Seeds**
1-509-964-7000
www.gardencityseeds.com
Potato, vegetable, and flower
seeds, including heirloom varieties.

Mt Tahoma Nursery
253-847-9827
www.backyardgardener.com
Rock garden and alpine plants.

Nichols Garden Nursery
1190 Old Salem Road NE
Albany, OR 97321
1-800-422-3985
www.nicholsgardennursery.com
Every kind of vegetable seed
imaginable, including many
unusual heirloom varieties, as well
as herb plants, citrus trees, olive
trees, strawberry plants, and
gardening supplies and tools.

White Flower Farm
167 Litchfield Road
Morris, CT 06763
800-503-9624
www.whiteflowerfarm.com
Offers a wide selection of
houseplants for the terrarium
project. Bulbs are another
specialty, as are lavender plants,
strawberries, and heirloom
tomatoes.

picture credits

2–3 Clothes from a selection at H&M (www.hm.com); trough from Ikea; plants from Ginkgo Garden Centre; wooden trowel from Neal's Nurseries; mini trug with tools from Habitat; plants from Woldens (www.betterplants.co.uk), Wyevale Garden Centres and Crews Hill Gardening Club (020 8367 9406); 4–5 burlap fabric for tote bag and plant labels from The Wimbledon Sewing & Craft Superstore; wooden trowel from Neal's Nurseries; 6–7 plant pots from Homebase; mini trug with tools from Habitat; annual plants from Homebase; 8–9 mini trug with tools from Habitat; 10–11 pots from Homebase; compost pots from Neal's Nurseries; clothes from H&M (www.hm.com); 12–13 rakes, gloves, spade, and dibber from Neal's Nurseries; mini trug with tools from Habitat; boots from a selection at Sainsburys and Woolworths; 14–15 rake and spade from Neal's Nurseries 16–17 spade and trowel from Neal's Nurseries; watering can from John Lewis; 18–19 glass jars from a selection at Muji (www.muji.co.uk); clothes from H&M (www.hm.com); seeds and tray courtesy of Martyn Cox; 20–21 terracotta pots from Homebase; paper potter tool from Nether Wallop Trading Company; paper for pots from Cowling & Wilcox (www.cowlingandwilcox.com); 22–23 terracotta pots from Homebase; plastic scissors from Early Learning Centre; 24–25 wooden dowel for scarecrow from B&Q; 26–27 watering can from John Lewis; star patterned beaker from Cath Kidston (www.cathkidston.co.uk); wood plant labels from The Wimbledon Sewing and Craft Superstore; 28–29 paper potter tool from Nether Wallop Trading Company; 30–31 windowbox and herbs from B&Q; 32–33 plastic scissors from Early Learning Centre; cellophane bag from Lakeland Ltd; gingham ribbon from The Wimbledon Sewing & Craft Superstore; 34–35 glass pots from IKEA; egg cups from John Lewis; large lollipop sticks from The Wimbledon Sewing & Craft Superstore;

36–37 metal wastebasket from IKEA; potting mix from J Arthur Bowers; potatoes from Thompson & Morgan; 38–39 woven hanging basket, plants, and herbs from a selection at Wyevale Garden Centres, Homebase and B&Q; potting mix by J Arthur Bowers; watering can from John Lewis; 40–41 strawberry planter from Homebase; strawberry plants from B&Q; watering can from John Lewis; clothes from H&M (www.hm.com); 42–43 star-patterned plastic beakers from Cath Kidston (www.cathkidston.co.uk); plants from Crews Hill Gardening Club (020 8367 9406); 44–45 cupcakes from Waitrose (www.waitrose.com); 46–47 terracotta bowl from Homebase; glass pots from IKEA; paintbrushes from The Wimbledon Sewing & Craft Superstore; compost from Homebase; 48–49 cacti from Neal's Nurseries; plastic animals and figures from Toys R Us (www.toysrus.co.uk); bowl and white gravel both from Homebase; 50–51 alpine plants from Browns Garden Centre (www.brownsgardencentre.co.uk); compost from Homebase; wooden cows from Just Williams; watering can from John Lewis; 52–53 terracotta pots from Homebase; grit from Wyevale Garden Centres; compost from Homebase; sempervivums from Crews Hill Gardening Club (020 8367 9406); 54–55 animals from Toys R Us (www.toysrus.co.uk); charcoal from Enfield Bird Centre; plants from Homebase/Wyevale Garden Centres; clay pellets from Homebase; potting mix from J Arthur Bowers; 56–57 bamboo stakes from B&Q; rake from Neal's Nurseries; 58–59 watering can from John Lewis; bamboo stakes from B&Q; 60–61 pot from Homebase; plants from Browns Garden Centre (www.brownsgardencentre.co.uk), Wyevale and Crews Hill Gardening Club (020 8367 9406); compost from Thompsons of Crews Hill (www.thompsonsofcrewshill.com); 62–63 felt, pipecleaners and miniature pompoms from The Wimbledon Sewing

& Craft Superstore; 64–65 terracotta pots and gerbera plants from Homebase; clothes from H&M (www.hm.com); 66–67 birdbox from Neal's Nurseries; lollipop sticks from Hobbycraft; 68–70 lollipop sticks from Hobbycraft; large lollipop sticks from The Wimbledon Sewing & Craft Superstore; 70–71 felt, miniature pompoms and pipecleaners from The Wimbledon Sewing & Craft Superstore; 72–73 flower press from Lakeland Ltd; plants from Ginkgo Garden Centre; basket from Neal's Nurseries; 74–75 terracotta saucer, pebbles, and waterproof adhesive and grout from Homebase; 76–77 raffia from Hobbycraft; 78–79 felt and pipecleaners from The Wimbledon Sewing & Craft Superstore; 80–81 burlap, fusible interlining, and embroidery thread all from The Wimbledon Sewing & Craft Superstore; 82–83 as above; wood plant labels from The Wimbledon Sewing & Craft Superstore; trowel from Neal's Nurseries; 84–85 loose lavender from The Norfolk Lavender Company; fabrics from a selection at Cath Kidston (www.cathkidston.co.uk); embroidery threads from The Wimbledon Sewing & Craft Superstore; clothes by H&M (www.hm.com); 86–87 bias binding and muslin for apron from The Wimbledon Sewing & Craft Superstore; fabric paint from The Stencil Library; watering can from John Lewis; basket from Neal's Nurseries; plants from Ginkgo Garden Centre; 88–89 glass jars from IKEA; beads from The Wimbledon Sewing & Craft Superstore; wind chime (used for pieces) from Tiger Lilly Flowers; 90–91 as above; 92–93 envelopes from a selection at Rymans; raffia from Hobbycraft; 94–95 brown paper from IKEA; raffia from Hobbycraft; card tags from Rymans; clothes from H&M (www.hm.com); 96–97 string from Homebase; birdseed from Neal's Nurseries; 98–99 wire from The Wimbledon Sewing & Craft Superstore; raffia from Hobbycraft; 100–101 colander from IKEA; clothes from H&M

(www.hm.com); 102–103 clothes from H&M (www.hm.com); pumpkin from Kennards Good Foods (57 Lamb's Conduit Street, London WC1N 3NB, 020 7404 4030); 104–105 wooden dowel for scarecrow frame from B&Q; burlap from The Wimbledon Sewing & Craft Superstore; 106–107 as above; 108–109 twig wreath from a selection at Tiger Lilly Flowers; gingham ribbon from The Wimbledon Sewing & Craft Superstore; 110–111 twig wreath from a selection at Tiger Lilly Flowers; gold and silver paint from The Wimbledon Sewing & Craft Superstore; gold ribbon from Hobbycraft; 112–113 silver paint from The Wimbledon Sewing & Craft Superstore; 114–115 boots from a selection at Sainsburys (www.sainsburys.co.uk) and Woolworths; 116–117 chocolate coins from Selfridges (www.selfridges.com); 118–119 bubble mixture from Tesco (www.tesco.com); 120–121 watering can from John Lewis.

index

Figures in italics
indicate captions

alpine garden **50–51**
animals, pine cone **70–71**
annuals, colorful **42–43**
aprons **13**
    printed **86–87**

backyard safari **122**
bacteria, harmful **13**
bamboo **11**
    teepee **56**, **57**, **59**, *59*
bananas **10**, **22**
beans **56**, *58*
bees *27*, **38**, **122**
birdbath, pebble **74–75**
birds **11**, *27*
    bird feeder **96–97**
    scaring **25**
boots **13**, *13*
butterflies *27*, **38**, **122**
butterfly basket **38–39**

cacti planter **46–49**
car wash **120**
carnivorous garden **60–61**
chard *59*
child's own patch **10**, **11**,
    14, *14*
chipmunks *27*
Christmas wreath **110–11**
clothing, protective **13**
composting **13**, **17**
containers
    choosing **43**
    and compact plant
        varieties **14**
corn *59*
crazy eggheads **34–35**
crystallized pansies **44–45**
cuttings *20*, **21**

daisy chains **76**, *77*
dead flower heads **17**, *19*
digital camera **122**

edible plants **22**
elephant ears **22**
elf house **78–79**
exotic plants, large-leaved
    10, **11**

explorers' kit **122**
fairy posies **76**
feeding **17**
fertilizers **17**
French marigolds **59**
funny face *24*

garden centers **17**, *19*,
    21, **22**, *22*
garden games **118–19**
gloves, gardening **13**, **48**
grasses **10**
gravel, decorative **48**

hanging baskets **17**
harvest wreath **108–9**
herbs
    harvesting **32–33**
    herb planter **30–31**
houseleeks **52–53**

jack o' lantern **102–3**

kitchen waste *16*

ladybugs *27*, **122**
lamb's ear **22**
lavender bags **84–85**
lawn **11**
    clippings **17**
lettuces **59**, *59*

mammals, small *27*
manure
    handling **14**
    spreading **14**, *16*, *56*
marigolds *59*
mini-beasts **11**, *27*, **122–
    23**
mulching **17**

nasturtiums **59**, *59*
necklace, seed **100–101**
nesting box, wooden **66–
    69**
nurseries **21**, *22*

pansies, crystallized **44–
    45**
peanut heart **98–99**
peas **56**, **59**
pest control **17**

pine cone animals **70–71**
plant bingo **116**
plant lists
    crazy fruit and
        vegetables **24**
    fast-growing seeds **25**
    giant's garden **26**
    nature's garden **27**
    plants for pots **27**
    salad bowl garden **24**
    scratch and sniff **26**
planting **21**
plants
    buying **21**, **43**
    choosing **22–23**
    plants to suit your
        garden **22**
    pot-bound **21**, **38**
    for pots **14**, **27**
    raising from seed **18**,
        19, *20*, **21**
    types of plants to buy
        22
    what not to grow **22–23**
play equipment **10**, **11**
poisonous plants **18**, **22**,
    23, *23*
potato planter **36–37**
potato printing **94–95**
pots
    painted **64–65**
    plants for **14**, **27**
    pot-maker device *20*
pressing flowers **72–73**
propagator **21**
prunings *16*, **17**

safety **10**, **11**
salad patch **56–59**
scarecrow **25**, **104–7**
scavenger hunts **116**
seed necklace **100–101**
seed packs, pretty
    92–93
seedlings
    repotting *20*, **21**
    water **58**
seeds
    collecting and storing *19*
    fast-growing **25**
    germination **18**, **21**
planting from seed **18**, *19*,

    35
sprouting **18**, *18*
slugs **17**, **59**, **122**
snails **17**, **59**, **122**
soil
    choosing plants to suit
        your soil **22**
    handling **13**
    preparing **14**, *14*, **16**
    raking **14**, *56*
    treading down **14**, *56*
spiders **122**
storing equipment **13**
strawberry planter **40–41**
succulent plants *20*, **21**
    succulent tower **52–53**
sun hats **11**
sunscreen **11**
suppliers
    124–25

terrarium **54–55**
tomatoes *58*
tools **11**, *12*, **13**
top tips on gardening with
    kids **11**
tote, burlap **80–83**
toxoplasmosis **13**
treasure hunts **116–17**
twig decorations **112–13**

Venus flytrap **60**

water painting **120**
water play **120–21**
water tag **120**
watering **17**
watering cans **17**, **58**
weeds **14**
whiteflies **59**
wildlife habitats **11**
wind chime, tin-can **88–91**
worm bin **17**
wreaths
    Christmas **110–11**
    harvest **108–9**

zucchini *59*

acknowledgments

Thank you to Polly Wreford for her beautiful photography and attention to detail. Thanks also to Iona Hoyle and Annabel Morgan for their help with all stages of the book—design, layout, and words.

Thank you to all the fantastic children who modeled for the book—for their patience during photography, and their enthusiasm for the projects they worked on.

Thanks also to the Norfolk Lavender Company for supplying the lavender, and to J. Arthur Bowers for supplying the potting mixes used in the projects.

Catherine Woram

Thank you Alis, Louis, and Lily.

Martyn Cox

Ryland Peters & Small would like to thank all the children who modelled in this book: Ahana; Bella; Carmel; Charlotte; Ella; Ella; Ivo and Honor; Georgia; Giorgia; Harry and India; Grace; Gregory; Harriet; Havana and Hassia; Isaac; James and Ben; James; Jessica and Anna; Jordan; Joseph; Kaan; Katie; Kinquaid; Lily; Louis; Miles and Caspar; Millie and Arthur; Sam and Roddy; Saskia and Mia; Sebastian and Oliver; and Tahiti.

Many thanks also to those who kindly allowed us to photograph in their gardens, especially Victoria Hutton and Patricia Woram.